The Art of
Flyfishing

The Art of Flyfishing

Brian Harris

Ward Lock Limited·London

Dedication

For Jean, for her forbearance as a 'fishing widow' for
more than twenty years, and for feeding fellow
fishermen at all hours; and for Stuart, for being
everything a fisherman's son should be – except better
than his father, which at times he is!
Thanks, too, to the many flyfishing friends, in Britain
and overseas, who have helped make my sport so much
more interesting and enjoyable, and to those who have
kindly given me fishing on their waters.

The author and publishers would like to thank the
following for kindly providing photographs for the
book.
Colour photographs:
Geoff Chesterman page 50 top; Nick Cranfield front
and back jacket, pages 50 below, 67, 101 top and
below, 102, 119 top: Trevor Housby page 119 below;
Neil Nevison page 120; Arthur Oglesby page 68;
John Tarlton page 49.
Black and white photographs:
Geoff Chesterman pages 17, 21, 22; Dave Collyer pages
23, 83; Nick Cranfield pages 6, 10, 15, 25, 27, 54, 56,
59, 61, 64, 70, 111, 114, 125; Roy Eaton page 139; Jens
Ploug Hansen pages 90, 103, 131, 134, 135; Brian
Harris page 128; Terry Hill pages 8, 13 top and below;
Neil Nevison pages 18, 41, 45, 46, 52, 104, 105, 107,
109, 150, 151, 160, 163, 166–169; Arthur Oglesby
page 96; Dave Steuart page 117; John Tarlton pages
75, 77, 78, 82, 85, 93.
Drawings and diagrams by David Oxford.

© Brian Harris 1980

First published in Great Britain in 1980
by Ward Lock Limited, 47 Marylebone Lane,
London W1M 6AX, a Pentos Company.

Layout by James Campus
House editor Helen Douglas-Cooper

Text filmset in Monophoto Garamond
by MS Filmsetting Ltd, Frome, Somerset

Printed and bound in Great Britain by Butler and Tanner Ltd, Frome and London

British Library Cataloguing in Publication Data

Harris, Brian, *b. 1937*
    The art of flyfishing.
    1. Fly fishing
    I. Title
    799.1'2   SH456

ISBN 0–7063–5915–1

Contents

Introduction

Flyfishing is just one of the many techniques fishermen use to tempt fish to take a hook into their mouths, after which the barbed point is pulled home and the fight begins, hopefully with the fish finally coming to hand.

To beguile fish into accepting the hook it is adorned with various feather fibres, animal hairs and furs, silks, wools, man-made fibres and shiny metallic silver or gold tinsels. The so-called 'dressing' of the hook aims to imitate, in form and colour, the many different types of animal life on which fish feed, from tiny insects the size of a small grain of rice, fished under the water or on the surface, up to imitations of small fish, maybe 7.5 cm (3 in) or more in length, fished under water. In addition, flies are dressed with garish materials or in basic black or white simply to trigger an involuntary and instinctive attack from the fish. The two main classes of fly are usually termed 'imitative flies' and 'lures'.

Unlike the lead-weighted float or legering tackle of the bait fisherman, or the medium to heavyweight metal, wood and plastic fish-imitating lures – spinners, spoons and plugbaits – of the fisherman who uses so-called spinning tackle, the fly has little weight. It cannot be cast on a thin nylon line, so the line itself must possess the weight necessary to flex the rod and project line and fly, to which it is linked by a fairly inconspicuous length of nylon monofilament, called a leader, to the fish. The heavy flyline, usually tapered to a slim tip, is projected by the fisherman in an unrolling airborne loop over the water, the leader unrolling, rather like the end of a whip-lash, to deposit the fly.

That, in essence, is the basis of fishing with an artificial fly. It is fairly simple, and the technique of the basic cast is not difficult to master, under competent instruction, in a few hours. And in spite of the stories of flyfishing's mystique that have been put about in the past, it is perfectly possible to learn to cast from scratch in the morning, and to land one's first fly-caught trout in the afternoon of the same day. I know, because I have helped several beginners to do just that.

But flyfishing may be developed from this simple basis into an extremely skilful and artistic form of fishing. Like many other well-established field sports, flyfishing is, at its best, conducted in a way laid down by traditions which involve it being practised within self-imposed principles, most of them

Anticipation. A still-water trout flyfisher awaits the evening rise.

based on the fisherman's respect for his quarry, even to the extent, at times, of making the quarry more difficult to catch than need be. As a parallel, one can reach the tops of some mountains by walking up the easy slope, but climbers deliberately choose the steep faces, just to overcome the challenge.

History has it that artificial flies were being used to catch trout by the Greeks in Macedonia before the birth of Christ, but flyfishing as we know it today, using a heavy line and flexible rod to cast the fly, has its origins in seventeenth-century England. Most flyfishing ethics and methods stem from trout and grayling fishing in streams, and vast numbers of books have been written by men who were captivated by the sport through the years. But mankind's so-called progress has had a devastating effect on the environment and today many of the rivers and streams on which flyfishing's early development occurred have been ruined by the three-pronged spear that has changed so many of the world's pure waterways to open sewers, or reduced their tumultuous and copious flows to mere trickles: pollution, land drainage and abstraction. Abstraction from boreholes, depleting the underground water which gave birth to many streams, has actually caused the complete disappearance of water in their channels!

As fewer rivers and streams were able to support trout, grayling and salmon, so the numbers of fishermen increased with the growing world population. The streams became overcrowded by fishermen and then riparian owners began to sell or lease the fishing rights to the highest bidders. The spiral in the cost of fishing had begun.

Many of the less wealthy flyfishers found prices of good fishing beyond their means, especially in rivers close to heavily populated areas. There has always been free trout fishing in the wilds of Scotland, the Welsh hills and in Ireland – there still is – but that did not help those who did not live there.

A superbly shaped brown trout from Rutland Water, Britain's largest man-made lake.

However, the demands from the increasing population for more water paradoxically helped to make flyfishing for trout attainable for more people. Reservoirs were built in which to store water in autumn and winter that could be released to maintain river flow for summer abstraction, and increasingly these reservoirs have been stocked with trout; the fishing, mostly restricted to the artificial fly, being let on a season permit or day permit basis.

Today, government policy in Britain ensures that maximum amenity use is made of reservoirs, and the water authorities of England and Wales have a responsibility to provide those amenities, including fishing on their reservoirs. And since they do not have to make a profit from providing trout flyfishing on these waters, but only need to break even, the costs are quite reasonable, although some would hold that about £4.00 for a day's sport is too much!

Since World War II, most of the innovations in flyfishing have developed from still-water fishing, since in Britain there is more of this available to the flyfisher of modest means. Some of the reservoirs are vast – the biggest at the time of writing, Rutland Water, being 3,100 acres in extent when full – and very often the amount of wind on these often exposed, vast man-made lakes makes casting difficult. Also, because they are often deep and fish in summer may seek these depths for comfort, the fisherman may need to get his line and fly down 9 m (30 ft) or more in order to stand a chance of success.

These particular circumstances have been overcome by the use of stiffer and longer flyrods, special heavy lines for long-distance casting from the bank, and equally specialized lines which sink to great depths very quickly, used mainly by fishermen in boats.

The trout in these big reservoirs have to be stocked on a regular basis, since there is little or no natural regeneration, unless there are suitable feeder-streams with gravel beds suitable for spawning; few reservoirs have such facilities. Trout are stocked at an average weight of about 450 g (1 lb) – the takeable size limit – and in many reservoirs they grow rapidly to far greater sizes than many rivers can support, due to the vast amounts of food available, both in the form of insects and crustaceans, and small fish. And while it is well known that very big fish, indeed trout up to 4.5 kg (10 lb) or so, may be landed on ordinary light flyfishing tackle, there is wide use today of powerful rods and thick lines and leaders on reservoirs, with these big fish in mind.

In my opinion, the way in which still-water flyfishing has developed has denigrated the real purpose of flyfishing, which is to capture fish on light-weight, sporting tackle, and has created a race of fish-hungry, heavy-handed anglers who, in many cases, have lost sight of what the sport is all about. Certainly there are times and places where reasonably robust tackle is needed to combat the conditions, but on the whole the majority of modern flyfishers use tackle on still waters – and have often carried their heavy gear back to the rivers, too – that is not only tiring and unnecessarily cumbersome to use, but also 'overguns' the fish they catch. It is rather like using a deer-stalking rifle to kill a rabbit.

But trout are not the only fish to be taken on the fly. In the wild rivers there are Atlantic salmon, returning to their birthplace to spawn from the Arctic seas where they grow fat and heavy on rich feeding; and seatrout, migratory

The author fishing for summer salmon on the Conway (Gwydyr Hotel Water), near Betws-y-Coed, North Wales. The pool is Geulan Goch.

brown trout that can reach 9 kg (20 lb), which also spawn in the clean, gravel-bedded streams, running into them from the inshore coastal waters where they have grown fast on the shrimps, prawns, sand-eels, sprats and other small fish of the rich, salt-water larder.

In slower-flowing lowland rivers, canals, lakes and ponds, there are coarse fish, so called, that will take a fly; some, such as roach, rudd, chub and dace, believing it to be an insect or a shrimp, others believing it to be a small and desirably edible fish, they being the pike and the perch, although both pike and perch will also accept insect-imitating and crustacean-imitating flies.

Finally, in a kind of no-man's-land between the game fish (trout, seatrout and salmon) and the coarse fish (roach, rudd, chub, dace, pike and perch) there is the grayling, a beautiful inhabitant of clean, fast-flowing rivers that has some of the physical characteristics of the gamefish – notably the small, fleshy adipose fin possessed by both salmon and trout – but spawns not with the gamefish, in autumn and winter, but with the coarse fish, in the period from March to May.

In my twenty-odd years as a flyfisher – I have fished in other ways for more than thirty-five years – I have caught all the species mentioned, and more, including many of the tropical game fish of warmer climates than Britain's. I hope in the pages that follow, that I may be able to pass on most of the aspects of flyfishing that have been important to me, those which I have learned from others over the years, and those which I have learned for myself in the years I have cast a fly into many different waters.

PART ONE

Brown and rainbow trout

Chapter One

Physical and behavioural differences

The brown trout (*Salmo trutta*) and the rainbow trout (*Salmo gairdneri*) are the two species most important to flyfishers in Britain and north-west Europe, and are also of prime importance in the other parts of the world where they are found; from Australia, Tasmania and New Zealand to North America, South America, the foothills of the Himalayas, the highlands of the African continent, and the many other lands to which man has transferred his favourite sporting species.

Brown trout are native to Britain, but rainbow trout were introduced from North America in the 1880s. Both are found in rivers and streams and in lakes and pools, but apart from one or two places, notably the little River Chess in Buckinghamshire, and the Derbyshire Wye, the rainbow is unable to spawn naturally in Britain.

Being native, the brown trout does spawn naturally, but only in suitable gravelly streams. In big lakes, both natural and artificial, it will run up any small streams to spawn, usually from November onwards.

Growth rate

Trout, both browns and rainbows, need reasonably pure, well-oxygenated water in which to live. Brown trout live the longest; up to thirty years has been known, although ten years is considered a good age. Rainbows seldom exceed five years of age, and full growth is attained in four years. Brown trout, on the other hand, can grow all their lives, although in the later stages that growth may be very slow.

Because rainbows are faster growing than browns, they are more popular with fish-farmers, who are able to rear them to a good size, for the table or for stocking fisheries, with less expenditure on food and labour. Raising enormous rainbows has become big business, and in Britain some fisheries, mainly small privately-run pools, are stocked with fish of 9 kg (20 lb) or more, and fishermen pay large sums to have the chance of catching them.

Because they live for longer, brown trout can achieve very heavy weights – a specimen of 22.6 kg (50 lb) from a Norwegian lake is on record – and most brown trout are wild-bred fish, whereas most rainbow trout, in British waters, have to be stocked on a yearly basis.

Trout grow only as fast as the food supply in the water allows. There is a

Above: These fish illustrate the fast growth that follows the opening of a new reservoir, and they contained both insects and worms from the freshly flooded land. The top two are browns, and the bottom two rainbows.

Right: Exmoor's Barle is a beautiful example of a moorland stream and its little wild browns can provide challenging fishing with the dry fly, even in late March.

belief, well substantiated, that truly rapid growth occurs only when a fish is in a big water, be it a river or lake, with plenty of space. In small moorland and mountain streams containing peaty, acid water, a mature brown trout might weigh as little as 85 g (3 oz) at four years of age, while a fish of the same age in an alkaline stream might weigh 680 g (1½ lb) or more.

Besides being cheaper to rear to a good size for stocking waters, the rainbow also possesses other characteristics that make it a popular choice for flyfishing. It can tolerate water of a less pure state than can the brown trout, and it is also happy in water temperatures well above 21°C (70°F), while the brown, although able to cope, and to feed, in this warm water for brief periods, prefers his environment to be 15–20°C (middle 60's F).

Behaviour

It is necessary to understand the different habits of browns and rainbows, and to use that knowledge in choosing when and where to fish, and how. For example, the brown trout likes a more leisurely life than the rainbow. In rivers, the brown takes up a position where it can lie comfortably, supported by the current, and have its food brought to it by the stream. It will root around in weed-beds and among stones for shrimps and nymphs, but seldom travels far from its chosen station or lie. In still waters, browns have to swim about a little more to collect enough food, but they usually choose an area of water with shallows close to a deep area, remaining in the deeps until such times as they feel the urge to feed, when they move to the shallows. Browns also do most of their heavy feeding during periods of low light intensity, that is, at dawn and dusk, and at night.

Compared to the brown, the rainbow is a skittish fish, full of wanderlust. It is also a shoal fish, whereas the brown is often solitary and becomes more so as it grows bigger, or older. Stocked alongside browns, as it often is in rivers, it accepts the less comfortable lies, out in the shallows, and tends to move up and down the stream, searching for food.

When it is stocked in still waters, the rainbow swims in shoals, usually of a size and travelling upwind. It is more inclined to take a fast-moving or garish fly than the brown, probably because it is used to snatching at food in competition with its shoal-mates. However, rainbows in lakes can also live alone, or in small groups, especially as they reach the age of three years plus.

Rainbows usually nip at the fly and often miss it or just give it a tweak, or they may get the point a fraction inside the tip of the mouth. If several takes are being missed, it is almost certain that the culprits are rainbows; as is often proved when a hooked fish leaps to show itself and promptly sheds the hook from its light hold!

Browns treat the fisherman's fly with more caution and are less likely to be fooled than are rainbows. But when a brown does make up its mind that the fly is just what it wants, and that all is well, it will normally take very firmly, so that the fly gets a good hook-hold in the mouth.

On the hook, rainbows tend to leap frequently and make long, fast runs near the surface, but they soon run out of energy and may be led to the net. A brown, on the other hand, although it will often leap as high as a rainbow and run as far and as fast, will more usually swim deeper in battle with the rod and

A big net on a long handle is best for netting a trout from a boat. Here a Bewl Bridge (Kent) rainbow is nearly safe.

shows more guile, making for underwater snags or weed-beds where it may snag the line and then shed the hook. Many flyfishers hold the view that the rainbow is a clown and that the brown is a crafty gentleman.

While I have had the most exciting battles on fly tackle with rainbows, the fish roaring away with 64 m (70 yd) of line from the shrieking reel, then leaping clear of the water several times, and I do have great admiration for them, I prefer fishing for brown trout because they present more of a challenge and a good, well-proportioned brown trout is a very handsome fish indeed.

Trout in rivers

In rivers, rainbows are more easily spotted in their open lies than are browns, which tend to lie in concealment. They are used to stock such famous chalk-streams as the Test and the Itchen, where once the native brown held sway, and they form the basis of the annual catch today.

Both species eat the same types of insects and crustacea but the brown is more likely to feed on small fish than is the rainbow.

Brown trout spawn in November and December, but the rainbow, which is now of mixed stock (some being spring-spawners and others spawning in the autumn), may be found in a spawning condition from the time that the normal trout season opens on 1 April until well into June, and then again towards the end of the fishing season, in late September and early October. Some rainbows do manage to shed ova and milt on the wave-swept gravelly shores of lakes, but it never produces offspring. Many hen rainbows re-absorb their ova, while many cock fish die after being in the water for a season. Brown trout in still waters with no spawning streams may also spawn on gravel shores, and sometimes this can be successful. Hen brown trout, also, can re-absorb ova, but some become egg-bound and die.

Trout in spawning condition – and that may precede the actual time when eggs and milt are ready to be shed by several weeks – are usually slimy, soft-flanked and highly coloured, and are certainly not good to eat. Cock fish of both species develop a kype or hooked lower jaw and become more highly coloured, with the silvery sheen becoming leaden. Hen fish become darker in hue prior to spawning, and if spawny rainbows of either sex are killed, they become dark.

Trout in still waters

In most still waters, a 1.3 kg (3 lb) trout of either species is considered a good fish, although many big waters can produce grown-on rainbows of 1.8 kg (4 lb) or so and browns to 2.7 kg (6 lb) or more. In a few rich waters these weights may be doubled. Grown-on fish, which may be stocked in lakes and reservoirs at about 450 g (1 lb) in weight and then thrive to become perfect, solid-fleshed bright specimens weighing 1.3 kg (3 lb) or so, should not be compared with the fat, flabby and usually dull-coloured giant rainbows of 6.8–13.5 kg (15–30 lb) stocked in small put-and-take fisheries. Rarely do these man-reared monsters put on any weight after being turned loose in the small pools, and they usually *lose* weight and condition. Seldom do they have perfect fins and tails, either; they are usually ragged and frayed at the trailing edges, due to confinement in large numbers in small stock-ponds and, maybe, to the fish nipping each other.

Some rich reservoirs produce excellent growth rates. For example, Grafham Water in the English Midlands grows rainbows stocked at a weight of about 450 g (1 lb) to weights of about 1.3 kg (3 lb) or more in about four months. The fish are stocked just before the season opens, and more are usually put in at intervals throughout the season in a topping-up exercise, depending on the number of fish being caught.

Good river feeding can grow rainbows stocked at around 450 g (1 lb) to 900 g (2 lb) or more by the end of the summer; a growing period of about five months. Rivers, unless suddenly polluted, having water abstracted from them, or suffering ecological disasters, remain fairly constant in their fish-growing properties, but still waters are not usually like that – at least, man-made waters are not. And it is on reservoirs that most trout flyfishing is done today, unless one is fortunate enough to live among the big, wild lakes of countries such as Scotland or Ireland.

Newly-flooded land, particularly well-farmed agricultural lowland, provides the stocked trout with an abundance of food. Worms and insects emerge from the flooded land, and worms in particular make for rapid fish growth. The fertilizers from the land are leached into the water in solution, and this rich mineral 'soup' helps the formation of weed-beds. The chalk and lime often used to dress the land increases the ability of the water to support many insects and crustaceans, and this alkaline water generally produces the best fish.

However, the worms are soon eaten, as are the ground grubs and insects. The water uses the rich run-off from the land and then, after some three or four years, the true natural character of the reservoir begins to emerge. Some, like Grafham Water, Chew Valley Lake and Blagdon in the English West Country, retain the ability to grow big trout, but most lose it.

Trout are stocked at about 450 g (1 lb) in weight and, in these established,

Opposite: Some reservoir trout fisheries can produce excellent fish, like this bag of six – a limit – weighing over 5.8 kg (13 lb), taken by the author from Bewl Bridge on nymphs.

average reservoirs, they may reach 680 g ($1\frac{1}{2}$ lb) or so over the period April to August. A few fish may not grow that fast; even fewer may reach 1.1 kg ($2\frac{1}{2}$ lb). The average weight of an English reservoir trout when caught is between 450–680 g (1–$1\frac{1}{2}$ lb).

In these reservoirs, stocked brown trout may remain uncaught for many seasons, and quite often browns of 3.6 kg (8 lb) or more turn up from these average waters. It is a matter of life-span and the brown's natural ability to make the best use of his environment. A big brown will probably have turned to a diet of small fish early on in its life, which helps it grow fast with the least expenditure of energy. When it decides to accept insects, it usually waits until there is an abundance of big ones, such as Mayflies, big sedge-flies, night-flying moths and, very important, craneflies (daddy-long-legs).

In recent years, water authorities have begun to put a few very big stock-fish into reservoirs – usually rainbows grown on high-protein food pellets in hatcheries, weighing 2.7–4.5 kg (6–10 lb) – and the capture of one of these proves rather confusing to fishermen. Sometimes it is difficult to tell if a fish of this size has grown from about 900 g (2 lb) in a number of seasons, or whether it is a stock-fish.

A still-water rainbow gently takes at the surface and turns down with its prize.

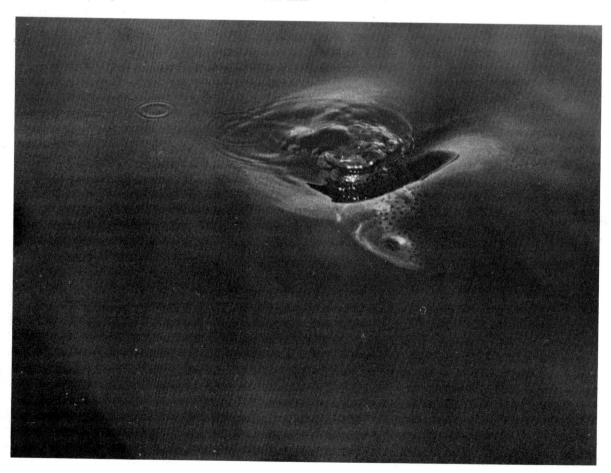

Seasoned flyfishers decry these big stock-fish and are not pleased if they catch one, because they are usually very easy to catch and, in spite of their size, do not fight as hard as a fish of 900 g (2 lb) that has reached that weight from 450 g (1 lb) when it was stocked earlier in the year. It is easy to see, however, why these big fish are being stocked: they create news and excitement in the popular angling press, and the reservoirs get more customers as a result of the publicity.

I know of one small reservoir which was once stocked with nine big rainbows, all around 2.7–3.6 kg (6–8 lb), in addition to the normal main batch of 450 g (1 lb) fish, one spring. Within five weeks, six of them (if I remember correctly) had been caught – and that water covers 180 acres! I hooked the sixth, of 3.2 kg (7 lb), and handed the rod to a friend I was teaching to use the flyrod. He brought it to the net in about two minutes, and it took no more than 4.5 m (5 yd) of line from the reel.

No matter what species of trout a river or lake contains, nor, to a large extent, whether those trout reach a maximum weight of 450 g or 3.5 kg (1 lb or 8 lb), catching them on a fly is always enjoyable. A 450 g (1 lb) trout from a tiny moorland brook, where the fish average three or four to that weight is worth a 1.3 kg (3 lb) one from an average reservoir, and indeed, a 6.8 kg (15 lb) one from a small put-and-take pool where all the fish are put in weighing 4.5 kg (10 lb) or more.

Chapter Two

Still waters, natural and artificial

Still water is a misnomer. No water is ever truly still. The surface of the smallest farm pond is ruffled by the wind, thus creating drift. On large waters, wind has a dramatic effect, not only building up large waves, but also creating quite swift currents in the water for up to a day after the wind has fallen. Temperature, too, has its effects, the cool water descending, because it is heavier, to be replaced by warmer water on the surface. Wind cools surface water and also blows it towards the lee shore. It sinks as it travels, causing a current down to quite a considerable depth. The water piles up against the lee shore, then runs back at a lower level.

Strange phenomena occur on still waters. Often, as evening approaches after a warm, windless summer day, it will be noticed, from the movement of a floating flyline, that a strong surface drift has begun; and for no apparent reason. The smooth water suddenly begins moving very fast, causing a big bow to appear in a line cast at a right angle to the bank. Since they like to swim against any current, fish will begin to rise, moving against this drift.

Fish location

To consistently catch trout in still waters, whether they are as big as 3,000 acres, or are two-acre put-and-take pools, it is necessary to understand the water, its bottom configuration, the position of weed-beds, inflows and outflows, and what effects changes in the weather have on the water and thus on its trout.

For example, trout, like all the species mentioned in this book, have no eyelids. To avoid glaring light, they must go deeper in the water or find shade from trees, weed-beds, high banks and other objects. Therefore, on days when the sun is bright and the water calm, fish are seldom seen or caught near the surface, except in shaded areas. Wind can break up the light rays by causing a ripple, in which case some surface activity and sport may be expected.

On a vast natural lake or reservoir, even a little wind can create sufficient ripple to break up the light. On a small pool, however, especially if it is encircled by trees or in a hollow (which many are), wind has little effect, and although the surface water may move, no real, light-scattering ripple is present. On a bright, calm day, then, one must expect to find fish in small pools in the deeper places, in troughs in the bottom, alongside weeds or under trees.

Opposite: This mountain lake, nearly 600 m (2,000 ft) up in wild Snowdonia, is several hours walking and climbing away from any vehicle track, but well worth the effort. It's name is Dulyn; dull its wild browns are definitely not!

The solution is easy: fish the fly deep, or in the shade, and you should be presenting the imitation to fish.

Fish location is not so easy in a big lake or reservoir. For a start, fish density is far lower than in a stocked small pool, and it is very unlikely that the trout in a big water will be scattered all through it, like currants in a well-mixed cake. In areas catching the wind, for example, on a bright day, some fish may be found swimming near the surface. In areas out of the wind, the calm surface is likely to be unmarked by rising fish. Again, find deep or shaded areas in the calm and fish deep, and it is likely fish will be encountered.

Feeding patterns

In lowland waters, big and small, especially on those where there are large areas of water with a depth up to, say, 6 m (20 ft), there is usually plenty of food for the fish, both on the bottom and in the weeds, and some, in the form of insects (and a few crustaceans), which moves from bottom to top, either hatching (in the case of some water-bred flies) or returning to the bottom (in the case of beetles, water-bred spiders, crustaceans and molluscs like shrimps and snails). Thus fish in such waters can find their food where light and temperature conditions are comfortable for them.

But what about a mountain lake that is close to 600 m (2,000 ft) above sea level? Such lakes are characteristically deep and the water is acid; and cold, remaining so until far into the summer, due to the altitude. Life in the depths is sparse and trout find the small amount of insect and crustacean life only around the shallow margins or over mid-lake plateaux. They depend to a large extent on insects being blown from the land on to the surface, by the wind which so frequently eddies and blows in such localities.

Brown trout inhabit these mountain lakes and they seldom attain weights of 340 g (12 oz), although there may be the odd big fish, perhaps of a few kilograms, that learned at a young age to eat its own kind – the so-called cannibal trout – and on that rich diet, outgrew the rest.

Trout from Dulyn taken by three fishermen in less than half a day, mainly on dry flies but also on small nymphs.

Tiny wild browns from Exmoor's Barle, caught on dry flies on 16 March, a day when it snowed.

The run-of-the-mill mountain and moorland trout in such lakes lie deep but come rocketing up from their lies to grab any flies that alight on, or are blown on to the water. The flyfisher, then, knowing this, successfully uses small dry flies, although imitations of sub-surface insect stages may be useful in the shallows.

A similar state of affairs exists in high altitude streams on rocky, peaty ground in mountains and on moors. Even in the month of March, when dry-fly fishing on the rich, lowland waters has not begun, since the fish are feeding deep on nymphs and shrimps, the little upland browns will come up for the fisherman's dry fly. I have had excellent fishing on Exmoor's Barle, among other similar streams, when the season had just opened, and snow flurries were falling.

Rich lowland lakes – even the ones described as 'average' – support a vast and varied food supply for trout when compared to the acid waters of high altitude lakes. Most lakes and reservoirs hold shrimps, snails, tiny mussels, various water beetles, such as the Corixa and the great diving beetle, spiders, mites and midges, sedge-flies and at least some species of the upwing flies, among which the most frequently seen are the Pond Olive, Lake Olive, Caenis, Sepia Dun and the great Mayfly itself. There are also sticklebacks and other coarse fish species which can provide food for big trout. Other lowland still-water food items for trout include damselfly nymphs, water lice, and crane-flies which get blown on to the water in late summer.

By far the most important food items for trout in such waters are the midges and the sedges. Their numbers far exceed any other types of insect on still waters and in their various forms during their life-cycle, they are available to the trout throughout the year. Rarely is the throat and stomach content from a stillwater trout examined without a preponderance of either midge pupae or sedge larvae (caddis grubs) or pupae being present.

Midges

The midges, of the non-biting variety (most of them being known as Chirono-mids), are members of the flat-wing family of flies. Their life-cycle is egg, larva, pupa and winged adult. The larva is the so-called bloodworm; that little red, green or amber worm-like creature that can be seen in ponds, ditches and even water-butts, swimming with figure-of-eight lashing movements of its agile body. The larvae live among mud and bottom debris, some building tube-type homes in the mud in which they live, others living free. The second stage – after hatching from the egg – is the pupa. This is a creature varying from as little as about 3 mm to 19 mm ($\frac{1}{8}$–$\frac{3}{4}$ in) in length and is popularly termed a 'buzzer', which is a misnomer. The adult winged fly, which is the final stage after the pupa, is really the buzzer, since they often hatch in their millions on calm summer evenings, and congregate in great swarms, like drifting smoke, over the banks and the water. In such numbers the movement of their wings creates a buzz that may be heard from several hundred metres away.

Midge pupae of various kinds and colours – the most commonly used artificials being black, blood-red, olive green, pale green, amber, orange/silver, grey and white – may be present from April to the end of October. Their bodies are characteristically hook-shaped and it is in this form that midges are most often imitated by fishermen, although there are some imita-tions of the larvae (bloodworm). The winged fly is rarely taken by the fish.

When midges are hatching – and this can occur at any time of the day or night, according to species, though warm evenings produce most activity – the pupae rise to the surface and move along, twitching, beneath it, until the wing case on the back splits and they climb free of the pupal case and fly away. At times when the surface is calm and the surface film has extra tension, pupae find it difficult to break through to hatch, the result being that the ascending hordes build up to vast numbers, hanging in the film, head-up, or moving erratically along beneath it. Trout always like easy feeding and many will make leisurely patrols among the multitude, often with their dorsal fins and tail-tips showing, sipping in the pupae as they swim. A good fisherman will make hay at such times. However, quite often fly selection is of the utmost importance, for the trout may be taking just one species (or colour or size) of pupa from among the many that may be present.

Flyfishermen often wrongly call midge pupae 'buzzers'. These are the real thing; a good hatch of midges at Grafham Water, in the Midlands.

Sedge-flies (caddis-flies)

Sedge-flies belong to the roof-winged flies, so called because their two pairs of wings form a roof shape over their backs when folded. They look like moths, except that the wings are covered with tiny hairs rather than tiny scales; another similarity is that they mostly hatch into winged flies just before or after dark. In America, sedges are called caddis-flies, and this seems to make more sense since they are called caddis grubs (or worms) in their larval stage.

The life-cycle of sedges is egg, larva, pupa and adult winged fly, as with the midges, but in the larval stage they form a far more important food source for still-water trout than midge larvae appear to do, judging from the results of thousands of autopsies. In many regions of the British Isles, trout fishing opens on 1 April, and many trout caught at that time, and in the following few weeks, will be found to have their stomachs packed with various sedges in their cases.

A few sedges do not make protective cases in their larval stage, but most British species do. There are about 200 British species and, like the midges, they vary in size. Also, the larvae build their cases from different materials and in varying shapes: sand grains, tiny snail and pea-mussel shells, small stones, twigs, bits of grass and the stems and leaves of weeds are among the materials used. The trout swallow the case as well as the larva, probably grabbing it as it crawls slowly over the bottom or up plant stems.

So, sedges (caddis) help feed the trout in winter and early spring, but they seldom begin to hatch into winged flies until about the middle of June; and hatches continue until late September. It is during this period that fly patterns which imitate pupae become useful to the fisherman. And naturally, patterns to represent the hatched, winged fly are also useful then. The latter is fished as a dry fly, on the surface, and is usually retrieved across the water to create a wake, which simulates the action of winged flies as they run and flutter across the water trying to become airborne.

Upwing flies

The upwing flies useful to still-water trout fishermen are few in number compared to the midges and sedges. The five species mentioned earlier in this chapter are the most common; the Mayfly, the largest of them all, being found on fewer waters than the others.

The life-cycle of the upwing flies differs from those of midges and sedges. It runs egg, nymph, dun and spinner, the latter two stages both being winged, of which, more later. These upwing flies are more often copied as nymphs than as winged flies by the still-water fisherman, and are fished beneath the surface, as are the larvae and pupae of midges and sedges.

Nymphs of upwing still-water flies are roughly carrot-shaped, have a hunch-backed look behind their heads where the wings are encased, and have two or three short tails. It is easy to become bogged down in attempts to imitate the various still-water upwing nymphs: two or three fly patterns in sizes from 16 up to 10 (long-shank hook) seem to be accepted quite well by the trout when feeding on these nymphs. One fly pattern, the Pheasant Tail Nymph, does the job of imitating several species, and others with body colours of olive green, grey and dirty white – the last representing the Mayfly nymph – will usually be sufficient to fill any gaps. Two or three dry fly patterns will cope with situations when fish are feeding on winged flies.

Other sources of food

Trout in still water, and the browns in particular, feed heavily at times on shrimps. Patterns to represent these, especially in the June–August period, are often effective fished near marginal weed-beds and inundated grasses. Snails, too, are eaten in quantity, especially by rainbows. Sometimes these are harvested from the lake-bed, but at times during hot, calm summer weather, millions of snails may rise to the surface and crawl along on the underside of the film, migrating to another area. Fly patterns must be carried to imitate these, and the same patterns, with their bulbous bodies and maybe with a few fibres of hackle to give some movement to the artificial, may be used to represent water spiders and beetles, which have a similar body shape.

At certain times throughout the trout season, other food items may temporarily divert the trout's attention from the staple diet. For example, damsel-flies are active between mid-June and late August and, specially on windy days when the waves wash them from among their harbouring weed-beds, these large insects in nymphal form are taken avidly.

On some moorland lakes, the heathered banks may produce hordes of small beetles known as Coch-y-bondhus, and an artificial of the same name is then a very necessary pattern to have. When wind blows swarms of flying ants on to a lake, an imitative pattern is essential, because the fish become pre-occupied with eating the ants. The same occurs with big falls of craneflies, already mentioned.

Lures

Big reservoirs can be rather disconcerting, especially to the stranger, and local advice about fish location is essential for those who make long-distance, infrequent visits.

Trout in lakes, particularly browns, will feed heavily on small fish at certain times of the year. The prey may be sticklebacks, specially in May and June when the fish shoal in the weedy shallows to build nests and breed, or the fry of other coarse fish species, notably roach, rudd, perch and tiny pike. Fry-feeding by browns usually takes place towards the back-end of the season, in late August and September, when the fry congregate in vast swarms in the margins.

It is at such times that very big browns may be caught, using long-bodied streamers and other flies which imitate small fish. It is the one time when the flyfisher, who normally uses small flies to imitate the food items on which

trout are currently feeding, can use lures and fish them to imitate the fry, still happy in his own mind that he is truly fishing imitatively.

Lures have been mentioned several times in this chapter. Newcomers to flyfishing may wonder what the term means. In essence, a lure is a larger, long fly, sometimes highly coloured, with lots of flashy tinsel on its body and long wings of hair or feathers, or it can be predominantly black or white. Lures, unless fished to simulate small fish, or maybe leeches or other creatures of similar size, are not meant to represent anything in nature. They are cast out, more usually using a sinking line, though sometimes on a floater, and are pulled back, often fast, but sometimes quite slowly; trout will accept them at all times of the season. And to the imitative flyfisher's horror, it must be admitted that they sometimes work more effectively than the most beautifully dressed and perfectly presented imitation of what the trout are feeding on at the time.

Many theories have been suggested about why these big flies can be so effective, although it must also be said that, at times, they will fail dismally when imitative patterns work well. Among these is the idea that the big, flashy lure moving at a fair speed, triggers an instinctive attack from the predatory trout. The trout is a territorial creature at times, particularly just before and during spawning (this affects rainbows more than browns, of course) and, seeing the lure as an interloper, attacks it, to drive it away, in the only way it knows how: by snapping at it with its jaws.

Whatever the reason, lures are here to stay and on big reservoirs they are standard flies for many boat fishermen, and for some bank fishermen who like to use big, strong rods, heavy lines, and to cast a long way. Lures, or any fly on a hook larger than, for instance, a size 8 long-shank, are banned on some of the smaller lakes and put-and-take fisheries. Whether it is because they can be so effective with, it may be claimed, only a little flyfishing skill, or whether the method of fishing them disturbs the water and the fish, as it sometimes can, these bans are steadily being imposed on more of this type of water.

In the lure's defence, however, it may be claimed that at least the fisherman has to cast the lure with a flyrod and flyline, which is better than using a spinning outfit, and requires more skill. Indeed, this is the dividing line between permitted methods and outlawed methods on most trout reservoirs: so long as the fly or lure is cast on traditional flyfishing tackle, it is all right. Certainly a lure, of feathered or hairwing construction, may be fished much more slowly, deep or shallow, with a flyrod and flyline than can most spinners, which are heavy and sink to the bottom if not retrieved at speed. And in this respect, as has been proved by experimental fishing on reservoirs, the 'long fly' is far more effective as a fish-catcher than the spinner.

Chapter Three

Tackle and accessories for still water

Still waters in which trout are found vary enormously. At the top end of the scale are the vast Scottish lochs and Irish loughs, the big natural lakes of the English Lake District, reservoirs such as Rutland Water, at 3,000-plus acres the largest (at the time of writing) man-made sheet of water in Europe, Grafham Water (1,600 acres) and others like Chew, Blagdon and Bewl Bridge. Waters like these are fished from the bank and by boat, with widely varying techniques being used.

At the lower end of the scale are the little pools, maybe only an acre or two, which are run as put-and-take fisheries, and there is a big middle ground comprising both mountain and lowland natural lakes and dams, varying from around fifteen acres up to perhaps a hundred acres or so.

The trout in these waters are as varied in size as the waters are, and to make the most of both the environment and the fish it is necessary to use a wide range of lines and rods. Notice that I put lines ahead of rods: in trout flyfishing the line must be selected before all else; it is the most important item of tackle.

Lines

In general terms, choose the lightest line that will do the job. A light line may be cast on the water gently; it sets up less resistance, from friction across and through the water, such as when a trout takes the fly and when it is being played, than a thicker, heavier line; and a light line on a light, slim flexible rod increases the enjoyment of playing the fish. The lightest flyrod obtainable is quite capable, in skilled hands, of bringing to net a trout of 4.5 kg (10 lb); and light rods are less tiring.

However, light flylines and toothpick rods have their limitations. One cannot expect to cast a big, heavy fly or lure vast distances on a light line; the line just has not got the weight to carry the big, air-resistant fly. Nor will a very light line cast easily into a strong wind; and if much sunk-line fishing is to be done, specially from a boat over deep water, a heavy, fast-sinking line will be needed, for a light sinking line will waste good fishing time – one has to wait too long before it sinks to a fishing depth.

Light lines and light rods are compatible with the essence of flyfishing, which is the use of skill, artistry and delicacy in outwitting the quarry. Using unnecessarily heavy lines or rods reduces delicacy, makes fishing for long periods more physically exhausting, and is parallel to buying a lorry to use as a family car; both will carry the family around, but the lorry is not necessary for the job.

It is easy to become bogged down discussing flylines. There need be only one criterion: will the chosen line cast the size of flies you need to use, on the water you plan to fish, and do so on a rod that is capable of being used by you for a long day?

For still-water trout fishing, line weights between size 3 and size 8 will cope with most situations. If you plan to do much boat fishing on big, deep reservoirs where large trout lie deep in the water for much of the time – waters like Grafham Water and Rutland, for example – you may need to have a size 9 fast-sinking line and a rod to match.

The Americans provided a weight-standard for designating flylines, and this standard is used all over the world today. It is known as the AFTMA code: American Fishing Tackle Manufacturers' Association; and is now shortened in Britain to AFTM: Association of Fishing Tackle Makers. It was worked out by weighing the first 9.1 m (30 ft) of the line, but excluding the final thin, level tip section, in grains, and then matching this weight to the flexibility of the rod. With 9.1 m (30 ft) of the right weight of line in the air, being cast backward and forward and then cast out, the rod should flex easily to propel the line, provided the handle of the rod is firmly anchored in the hand (rather like the schoolboy trick of jamming a wooden ruler in a crack in the desk-top and bending it back with a piece of inky blotting-paper held on its tip – let the tip go and the ruler straightens, projecting the missile towards the unfortunate victim).

However, since most Americans fish rivers by choice, the 9.1 m (30 ft) of line was chosen to represent the average amount that needed to be projected back and forth to make a 13.7 m (15 yd) cast, the remaining length of line being drawn through the rings from coils hanging or held below the butt ring, by the 9.1 m (30 ft) travelling forwards. A 13.7 m (15 yd) cast is certainly adequate for much river fishing for trout, and sometimes for small still waters, but when fishing big reservoirs and lakes it is necessary to be able to cast up to 22.8 m (25 yd) regularly with a full, double-taper floating flyline, and to place line and fly down like gossamer, and with accuracy. And it is not possible to attain such distances with only 9.1 m (30 ft) of the line in the air. In fact, 18.3 m (60 ft) will need to be cast back and forth, the other footage being shot through the rings from the spare loops or coils below the butt ring.

It therefore follows that instead of matching the weight of 9.1 m (30 ft) of line one needs to use, for example, a rod suitable for casting up to 13.7 m (15 yd) with a size 6 line, to cast 22.8 m (25 yd) with a size 4 line when very long casts are necessary. The extra weight of the 18.3 m (60 ft) of lighter line in the air while casting is approximate to the 9.1 m (30 ft) or so of size 6 line.

Since this book is intended to be read by beginners, as well as flyfishers who have had some experience, it is necessary to delve at least a little way into flylines and the different types suitable for still-water trout fishing.

The most widely used is the double-taper line. This is usually 9.1 m (30 yd) long, level in the centre, with 2.4–3.6 m (8–12 ft) tapered at each end. In trout fishing, the double-taper line is mainly used floating, or with the centre part floating and both tips sunk. It may be turned round on the reel when one end becomes cracked and worn, so extending its useful life. Because of the drag of the heavy centre section in the rod rings, this line's tip turns over more precisely, so that it unrolls smoothly over the water and permits the angler to set the fly and leader down delicately. It can be used to cast an average of 18.3 m (20 yd) or so, although a skilled flyfisher can often get the whole 27.4 m (30 yd) out over the water.

For making consistently long casts, a weight-forward line may be used. This consists of a front section similar to the front 9.1 m (30 ft) of a double-taper line but with the line then suddenly becoming thinner, over 90 cm 2.4 m (3–8 ft), down to some thin, level shooting line, in diameter approximately that of the fine level tip of the double-taper line. When casting the weight-forward line, only the thick front 9.1 m (30 ft) or so are projected outside the rod tip, and the cast is made to send the heavy front section out at speed, dragging the slim, shooting line, which has less resistance in the rod rings than the thick centre section, or belly, of the double-taper line, behind it.

The weight-forward line makes regular casting distances of 22.8 m (25 yd) reasonably easy, but the use of this type of line demands additional skills in casting, since it is necessary to project the heavy front part of the line at high speed, generally at a higher elevation than a double-taper line needs, to attain the ranges of which it is capable. The double taper can be *floated* out, and the weight-forward line will never land as gently as the former, since all its casting weight is concentrated near the end and the thin shooting line has little resistance in the rod rings.

Some weight-forward lines are 27.4 m (30 yd) long, as are the double tapers, but variations are made to meet different fishing requirements. For example, there is the long-belly weight-forward line, in which the heavy front section is usually about 12 m (40 ft); 3 m (10 ft) longer than the normal line. The idea of this longer belly section is to permit short-distance casts to be made with some of the thick line still inside the tip ring of the rod, so providing the resistance and delicacy of the double taper. Another reason for the extended belly is that most flyfishers cannot contain themselves to just having the first 9.1 m (30 ft) of a normal weight-forward line outside the rod tip, and by 'over-

Flyline profiles

DOUBLE TAPER (usually 27.4 m/30 yd)

level tip   level belly   level (spare) tip

WEIGHT-FORWARD TAPER (27.4-32 m/30-35 yd)

level tip   level belly   level dressed shooting line

SHOOTING TAPER (9-13.7 m/10-15 yd)

level tip   level belly   glued splice

thin braided monofilament nylon shooting line

lifting', as the fault is termed, they cause excessive wear on the portion of thin shooting line just behind the belly. The fault is due to trying to attain distance beyond one's normal capability, through brute strength.

Weight-forward lines are made to float throughout their length, or to sink over the final 3 m (10 ft) or so, but with the rest of the line floating, or to sink completely – slowly, quickly, or very quickly.

The type of line that can be cast farthest of all – and that means fastest as well – is the shooting taper or shooting head, as it is more commonly known. In essence, the shooting taper is like the weight-forward line except that, instead of the shooting line behind the heavy front belly being vinyl-coated braided nylon or Terylene it is of either nylon monofilament, round or oval in section, or of braided strands of nylon. Both are very much thinner than the dressed line on the weight-forward taper, and because they are thinner and have smoother surfaces, they slip through the rings of the rod, and through the air, much more quickly and easily. The competent performer with a shooting taper will consistently cast 32 m (35 yd) or more in favourable conditions; and with a following wind and no obstructions behind, 45.7 m (50 yd) is possible.

However, such lines cannot be made to alight with delicacy on the water regularly. They tend to fold back on themselves, because of the absence of friction, instead of unrolling in a loop as does the double-taper line.

Shooting tapers are very useful to the lure fisherman, who needs to cast a long way with a minimum of backward and forward rod movements. They are at their best as sinking lines, because once they are on the water as floaters, there is nothing the fisherman can do to control them, except pull them in. The double taper may be controlled in a number of ways, due to the weight of its belly section, which can make fishing in windy weather more effective.

However, shooting tapers of floating line are useful, more particularly to the reservoir bank angler on hard-fished waters where, quite frequently towards the middle and back-end of the season, fish become very wary of coming too close to the margins, having seen too many lines and flies cast by too many fishermen. Then, the man with the floating shooting taper who can cast 27.4 m (30 yd), whereas most of the other bank anglers cannot reach much more than 18.3 m (20 yd), may catch most of the fish.

Most fishermen make their own shooting tapers by cutting them from double-taper lines and knotting, splicing or glueing the shooting line to the back end, although half lines are sold in the shops.

The properties of the line – floating, sinking, sinking-tip – plus the profile of the line when lying on the ground and viewed from above – double taper, weight forward or shooting taper – are signified by an internationally accepted key. Double taper is DT, weight forward is WF and shooting taper is ST.

Further, the properties of the line are also shown by another key. A floating line is signified by the letter F, a sinking line by S, and a line that floats but sinks at the tip or tips, is a floating/sinking line – F/S. Some lines are made that sink very slowly when used straight out of the box but can be made to float with a light smear of grease. Such lines are known as intermediate density lines and are denoted by the letter I. They are very rarely made or used.

The code of figures which describes the various weights of flylines begins at 1 and goes up to 12, as a rule, although there are heavier lines than a 12, made for some aspects of deep-water tropical flyfishing with flies that may be 20 cm (8 in) long. For most flyfishing on still water a size 6 or 7 floating double-taper line will do the job. For really delicate presentation and the ability to see takes and lift into them like lightning, a floating DT 3 or 4 line is a revelation. And since it is used on a very slim wand of a rod, very fragile leaders may be used, with tiny flies, and the flex in the rod and the lack of friction of the thin line in the water permits big fish to be handled.

Many still-water flyfishers will scoff at the idea of using a size 3 or 4 line. They think it will not cast far enough, but the real truth is that 95 per cent of them have never even tried such a line and matching rod, and cannot therefore judge. Certainly I use size 3 floating lines only when conditions are reasonable – and immediately detect the benefit of their use in better catches – but my son used such a line, even in force 6 winds, for at least 80 per cent of his fishing during the season of 1979, and his catches exceeded mine, and those of most other anglers on the water, by nearly 100 fish. Once one gets used to using the light line and matching rod, one can learn little tricks that will beat wind and other problems. Remember, always, that it is the speed of the line that counts when after distance. A light line at high speed may be cast 27.4 m (30 yd), the flyline-backing splice going up the rod rings, in good conditions; that is, with a gentle breeze from the side or from slightly behind.

A light line, however, loses velocity more quickly than a heavy line because it lacks the mass to carry. It is the same with bullets: a heavy bullet may start more slowly than a light bullet, but the heavy one will still be travelling fast at a time when the light one has lost velocity and is being dragged down by gravity.

I seem to have written at length about flylines, but it really is important to understand them and choose wisely. Most of my still-water trout fishing is done with three lines: a DT3F, a DT6F and a WF7F/S. I used the DT6 most during the 1979 season, but that was because the rod to match the DT3 was not really suitable. Now I have a really good rod for the DT3, it has been used for most fishing this past season.

I do have a WF8F line, one with a 12 m (40 ft) belly, and I use this when a gale is blowing and I wish to fish a surface fly, such as a Muddler Minnow, across the waves at speed. I have also used it to good effect on damp evenings towards the back-end of the season when the atmosphere makes long casting with most other lines – except shooting tapers – almost impossible. Lines seem to stick to the rod itself and to the rings. Many anglers appear to have this problem all the time, but few bother to analyse the reasons for it.

Flylines vary widely in quality. Some companies make good floating lines, but bad sinkers, and vice versa. I would recommend Cortland's 444 as the best floating line, with the Air Cel Supreme and Masterline Chalkstream and Chancellor lines close behind. The best sinking lines are Scientific Anglers' Wet Cel, Shakespeare's International, with Masterline's Don close behind.

Sink-tip lines (F/S) are notoriously difficult to cast well, due to the sudden change in density of the two materials necessary to float the back end and sink the tip, but Masterline's grey Oxbridge and their fluorescent orange Chalk-stream, with a black sinking tip, seem to work better for me than others.

Flylines are made in many colours and I favour highly visible floating lines, which show me by their movement when a fish takes my sunken fly. Fluorescent orange is my favourite, white my second choice. Some fishermen feel that fish can see such bright lines, but I use long nylon leaders to keep my fly well away from the line and I took 538 trout on such a fluorescent line in 1978.

For sinking lines I like dark grey, green or brown.

Flylines are expensive items – £12–£15 for a good one at the time of writing – and they should be carefully maintained to last and perform well. All modern vinyl-coated lines must be kept clean, by wiping down after every trip with a soft cloth or paper tissue damped with fresh water. Some manufacturers provide a tin of cleaner and conditioner. Line coatings are damaged by cracking, mainly because they are whip-lashed when casting, although treading on them in boats, on hard banks, or using them coated with particles of grit will also cause damage.

Oil-derived chemicals also damage lines. Prolonged exposure to strong sunlight should also be avoided: for example, do not leave the reel in the back window of a car for weeks on end.

Next in importance after the flyline is the nylon leader, but I intend to deal with leaders later on. It is now time to consider still-water flyrods.

Rods

As I have already said, most British still-water flyfishers use rods that are too long and too stiff, believing, quite wrongly, that such rods will cast farther and catch them many big fish. Rods, reels, lines and flies do *not* catch fish: the person using them does that.

Because a certain group of influential flyfishermen, with platforms in the fishing media from which to preach, have said that long, stiff rods and size 8–10 lines are necessary to fish successfully, most flyfishers have religiously followed their doctrine. The popular conception of a still-water trout rod is one of at least 2.75 m (9 ft) and up to 3.20 m (10½ ft), stiff enough to cast a size 8 or 9 line. Such combinations hopelessly overgun most trout (and trout fishermen), so that the person is exhausted in an hour or so and any fish he catches can show comparatively little fight. I have successfully used such rods and lines to catch Mexican tarpon up to 8 kg (18 lb), and American fishermen regularly catch salmon and big saltwater fish on what British fishermen might describe as 'a standard trout rod'.

I frequently use flyrods of 2.45–2.60 m (8–8½ ft) and weighing 70 g (2½ oz) for reservoir trout fishing with lines size 5 or 6. My rod for the size 3 lines is 2.60 m (8½ ft) and weighs 65 g (2¼ oz). My longest and strongest rod is 2.75 m (9 ft) and casts a DT7 or WF8 line. I use the latter about half a dozen times in any season. All three rods are graphite, or carbon fibre; I shall use the word graphite to describe such rods in these pages.

The important point about any flyrod is that it should suit the user's physique, ability and his personal whim. I have used other men's favourite rods and winced. They have tried my own prized possessions and handed them back with much headshaking.

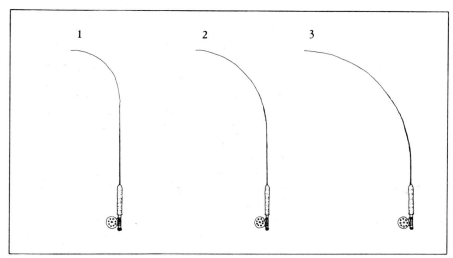

Types of flyrod action
1 Tip (fast) action.
2 Middle-to-tip (medium) action.
3 Through (butt) action.

If you can afford them, graphite rods are by far the best for still-water trout fishing. The reasons for this are that they are lighter than hollow glass-fibre or split bamboo cane, and therefore less tiring to use. They are thinner, and therefore have less wind resistance when casting and when fishing in a gale. The material recovers from bending more quickly than glass or cane, and having done so it does not continue to wobble, so, since the flyline in the air follows every movement of the rod tip, the graphite rod casts a straighter line than either of the other two materials.

I now like a crisp action in my flyrods. Ten years ago I tended to like rods that were floppier, bending down to the cork handle when casting, but graphite was not then available.

Hollow-glass rods are much cheaper than graphite and the better ones fish very well indeed. Until recently the main problem with the material was that, to get the crisp but smooth action, it was necessary to have a very thick tubular section near the handle – very ugly and presenting great wind resistance. Modern constructions in glass have avoided much of that problem.

Cane rods are beautiful – or the best ones are – but in lengths above about 2.45 m (8 ft) they can be too heavy for constant still-water use.

If I did more flyfishing from a boat on lakes and reservoirs, I would have a 3.05 m (10 ft) graphite rod with a fairly easy action matched to a DT5 or 6 line, but I cannot get really interested in boat fishing, and I recently sold my American rod of that length to a friend whose need was greater than mine.

Graphite rods by Shakespeare, Sue Burgess' 'Diamondbacks', Hardy 1978 'Graphite Carbon', Orvis, Thomas and Thomas, and Lamiglas have proved their worth. In the UK, Lamiglas produce many rod blanks for building at home and several British firms use them to make excellent rods. The first three named are my personal favourites, but some Bruce and Walker English graphite trout rods are excellent, too.

Bruce and Walker and Hardy also produce superb hollow-glass trout flyrods for still-water work. Some of the more rigid style rods by Carrol-Macmanus (blanks only) are also very good.

Cane rods by Hardy, Clifford Constable, Ken Johnson of Ballyduff in Ireland, Chapman of Ware, and Sharpes of Aberdeen are very reliable. Many American cane rods are superb.

While it is the blank, or shaft, of the rod that is its most important part, whatever it is made from, the quality of the rings, cork handle and reel-holder must be good, otherwise the rod will soon fail. For example, a set of poor quality rings can be grooved in two days of fishing by the abrasion of the line.

Tip and butt rings must be of very hard material, since they have to take abrasion from the line at various angles. Only rings with a hard-chromed surface, or of tungsten-carbide, or lined with aluminium oxide are suitable. For the intermediate rings I consider no other design than the snake ring, with a hard-chrome finish. Such rings are lighter than other designs, such as the single-leg Fuji rings that are lined with aluminium oxide, and may be whipped to the rod much more firmly.

It is folly to pay between £30 and £100 for a rod, which may be beautifully built and finished, only to have to take off the rings after a few months and renew them.

Cork handles should be hard and fairly slim, although the thickness of the handle should match the size of the fisherman's hands. Thick ones may be sanded down to suit. I have never felt the need for screw-type reel seats on flyrods, and favour a fixed clip at the extremity of the handle with a sliding ring to hold the reel's front foot. The parallel part of the handle to which the reel is fitted may simply be the cork, suitably reduced in diameter, or a section of hardwood, drilled and glued on to the rod butt, on which the clip and ring are fitted.

The joints of hollow-glass and graphite rods are usually of the spigot type, in which a reduced thick-walled tube of the rod material – or even a solid piece – is glued into the upper end of the butt section to fit into the open end of the tip section. There are variations on this, in which there is an enlarged section on the tip section to accept the butt, or a similar thicker piece on the lower section into which the tip fits. Spigot or similar joints should not fit together so well that the two halves of the blank touch when the rod is assembled; a gap of about 6 mm ($\frac{1}{4}$ in) allows for take-up over the years when wear reduces the comparatively soft, mated materials. This abrasion-induced wear may be retarded by rubbing the male part of the joint with a candle, thus coating it and preventing contact between the soft materials. But the wax should be removed periodically, with white spirit, and then renewed, to avoid the build-up of abrasive grit.

Cane rods are usually joined by metal ferrules, of brass, chemically turned a bronze or blue colour, or of nickel silver, similarly coloured, although some are left silver. The latter ferrules are best and more expensive. Again, they should not mate fully, but a gap of about 3 mm ($\frac{1}{8}$ in) should show on the connected sections of a new rod, to allow for wear. They should be kept clean and very lightly wiped with olive oil – not a mineral oil – before assembly.

It is quite unnecessary to pay a rod factory to make up a rod these days. Blanks of all three materials, most of them fitted with spigot or ferrules and some with the handles and reel fittings also put on, are widely available today

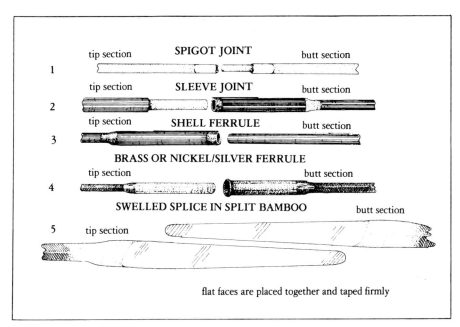

Flyrod joints
Joints 1–3 for hollow glass-fibre and hollow graphite rods. Joints 4 and 5 for solid split bamboo rods (were used for greenheart rods).

in most good tackle shops specializing in flyfishing. All that remains for the fisherman to do is to buy a suitable set of rings, some fine nylon whipping thread and some elastic yacht varnish. The rings may be put on in about three hours, the foot on each one being filed to a sloping feather edge with a small sharpening stone beforehand. This prevents an unsightly bulge and avoids the danger of the thread becoming worn. The ring is held in position on the rod blank by binding down one foot with adhesive tape, afterwards removing it to whip down that foot.

One can save nearly half the price of a factory-made rod by buying the parts and assembling them in a couple of evenings. When graphite rods cost about £70–£120, ready made, the saving is considerable – enough, almost, to make up two rods for the price of one ready-made one.

A point worth mentioning is that whippings should be started on the rod surface, then the turns of thread should travel up the slope of the ring foot; this prevents the turns slipping downhill, which would happen if it was done the opposite way. Turn the rod as the thread is applied tightly, and guide each turn to butt up to the preceding one. The number of turns round the rod and over the end of the thread, to lock it firmly, need be no more than four – long whippings are unsightly on a slim rod and may stiffen it. Varnish is applied directly on to the thread when all rings have been whipped on. At least three coats should be applied with a 6 mm ($\frac{1}{4}$ in) flat sable brush, but the first one should be smoothed and rubbed in well with the forefinger, to get the varnish to penetrate right through to the rod surface, and to flatten any projecting fibres of the thread.

When the final coat of varnish on the whippings is dry and quite hard, two final coats may be applied over the whole rod, including the whippings. Varnish is best applied in a dust-free room at a temperature of about 21 °C (70 °F), using the forefinger to apply it to the rod blank itself, working between two rings at a time. A brush is used to get under the rings and smooth round the whippings for a glass-like finish. Some fishermen like a dull finish on their flyrods, believing that the flash of a moving rod in the sun can frighten fish. I have never found this to be the case, but a matt finish may be obtained, once the final varnish coat is hard – after several weeks of drying – by gently rubbing it with pumice powder on a soft, damp cloth.

Reels

Reels for still-water flyfishing should be as light as possible and between 82–88 mm ($3\frac{1}{4}$–$3\frac{1}{2}$ in) in diameter. Single action or multiplying reels are suitable; automatic recovery reels are not – the only model with sufficient line and backing capacity is too heavy at 255 g (9 oz), the rest are too small.

Reels with perforated drums are best. They are lighter, since there is less metal in them, and the holes allow water to drain from the line and its backing after use. Many flyfishers hold the view that the reel is unimportant: that provided it holds the line, it will do. That may be so for those who fish with stiff rods, heavy lines and thick leaders, but when one goes out to fish for big trout with leaders as delicate as 700 g ($1\frac{1}{2}$ lb) test, the reel becomes a very important part of the tackle.

It must have a very smooth-running check or ratchet mechanism, preferably with an adjustable spring to apply more or less pressure to the running fish as it drags line from the reel. Any jerky motion from a reel with a roughly cut or large-toothed ratchet wheel can cause breakage of slim nylon leaders, or tear out the little hook, or break or distort the fine steel wire of the hook.

I like high quality reels: Hardys' 'Marquis' range are very good, as are some other Hardy reels, such as the new 'Sunbeam'. The very expensive Orvis 'CFO' is also excellent. All these have drums with exposed rims, on which manual pressure may be applied against a running fish approaching trouble, such as a sunken snag or weed-beds. Other reels also have excellent check mechanisms but have the rim of the drum running inside the frame of the reel, and manual pressure may then only be applied by putting a finger between the sideplates of the drum and onto the line itself. This is somewhat tricky and less delicate than a smooth rim of metal.

A much cheaper reel with an exposed drum rim is the English Intrepid 'Rimfly'. It is not made to the fine tolerances or finish of the Hardy and Orvis reels, and has a rather coarse ratchet mechanism, but it does sterling service, and a little molybdenum disulphide grease, such as MTS 1000 by Rocol, will smooth it out quite considerably. It is perfectly adequate for use with leaders of 2.2–2.7 kg (5–6 lb) test, and using such leaders I have used the reel to subdue bonefish and other fast-moving species on the tropical flats of Mexico and the Bahamas. A reel that can handle fish that run 90 m (100 yd) much faster than a man is not to be disregarded.

Each rod you own needs a reel to go with it containing a matching line; if lines that float, sink or have sinking tips are to be used on the same rod, then spare spools for the reel containing those lines can save extra expense in buying more than one reel. In practice, however, a lightweight rod with size 3 or 4 line will seldom be used for anything but a floating line; sink-tip lines of those sizes are seldom available, sizes 5–6 being the lightest. A rod for a size 6 line might well have a reel with spare spools for floating, sinking and sink-tip lines, however.

Splicing lines

A flyline, as I have said, may be 27.4–32 m (30–35 yd) in length, and in most situations, trout in still water will be landed with that length of line. However, some trout, and not necessarily huge fish, either, may make long, fast runs. I have had fish of less than 900 g (2 lb) take 64 m (70 yd) of line, then make a similar length of run after being reeled back to within a few metres of my position on the bank. Such long runs are rare, and the stories one hears of fish tearing 90 m (100 yd) of line from a reel are mostly exaggerated.

But having a reserve of line, especially when 'living dangerously' with delicate tackle, is a great comfort and may prevent the loss of the fish of a lifetime. For that reason, it is necessary to attach at least 45.7 m (50 yd) of thin but strong waterproof backing line to the rear of the flyline itself before winding it all on to the reel. The junction must be smooth, so as to cause no hitches as it is dragged up through the rod rings at speed by a fish, or when the fish is being reeled in and the joint hits the rod's tip ring. Since modern vinyl-coated flylines have a braided nylon or Terylene core, it is possible to join them to similar backing line of 5.4–9 kg (12–20 lb) test by gluing one inside the other.

Use a cyanoacrylate glue (such as Super Glue 3 in the UK). It is tricky to use because it sets in seconds and can glue human skin together, but, properly used, it has never let me down. About 5 cm (2 in) at the end of the flyline can be dipped in cellulose thinner (nail polish remover), and after about a minute it is possible to strip off the softened plastic coating with thumb and finger nails. The end of the line is then pulled inside the backing braid with a slim needle and the adhesive applied in tiny drops.

Alternatively, monofilament backing may be threaded with a needle into the back of the flyline, without the plastic being removed, and brought out again about 9 mm ($\frac{3}{8}$ in) up the flyline. Pull about 2.5 cm (1 in) out of the side of the flyline with the needle and remove the needle. Anoint the projecting backing, then pull back immediately. The glue sets instantly and the joint will be sound. Trim off any tag ends with a razorblade and cover the joined area with liquid vinyl (such as Vycoat) which is sold by tackle shops for such purposes. Splicing is illustrated on page 166.

Never, ever, be tempted to join backing to flyline with one of those plastic bobbin-shaped devices sold for this purpose. They will jam in the rod rings, especially at the tip ring where the line forms an angle.

When making up shooting tapers from double-taper lines cut off at the appropriate point, the same joint can be used to fit the nylon monofilament backing into the flyline. Simply cut a feather edge on the end of the 9–13 kg (20–30 lb) test nylon with a razor blade or scalpel, holding the line flat on a block of wood or cardboard, thread it through the needle and carry on as before. For attaching braided nylon, such as Shakespeare 5000 or Gudebrod Bass Line, in 11.3–13 kg (25–30 lb) test to a shooting taper, strip the flyline cover as before and pull this inside the hollow braid of the shooting line, bringing it out about 12 mm ($\frac{1}{2}$ in) back. A few drops of the adhesive will penetrate the open braid of the shooting line onto the flyline core and a superb joint results.

Sometimes when making this joint with braided nylon shooting line, the braid will unravel when the needle pushes it apart. This may be avoided by heating a small sewing needle, held in forceps or pliers, to cherry-red, then passing it round the braided nylon while it is on the thicker needle. The heat melts the braid, which rapidly cools into a solid state again, thus stopping further unravelling. Remove the shooting line from the big needle, trim off the ragged ends, then re-insert the needle and pull the flyline core through.

Leaders

Now for the leader. A very important part of the tackle, as I said earlier.

Until 1977 it was difficult to purchase a knotless tapered nylon leader longer than about 3 m (10 ft), but in 1977 Normark Sport introduced to Britain knotless tapered leaders of about 4.9 m (16 ft), with tippet tests of 1.3 kg, 2.2 kg and 3.1 kg (3 lb, 5 lb and 7 lb), and these have proved excellent for most forms of still-water work, although they are too long for most dry fly fishing, where 2.7–3.6 m (9–12 ft) is more manageable.

The leader has to do many things: first and foremost it forms a comparatively invisible link between the thick flyline and the fly, which encourages the trout to take the offering; it places the fly, and itself, gently on the water, being more slender and lighter than the flyline tip; and its length may be used, varied by the use of grease (to make the nylon float) or some form of detergent (to make it sink) to fish the fly slowly at any depth between 12 mm ($\frac{1}{2}$ in) sub-surface to maybe 6 m (20 ft) down. To do the latter task, of course, the leader must be more than 6 m (20 ft) in length. The thick butt end of the leader, attached to the tapered flyline, forms a continuous taper from line to fly and so turns over above the unrolling loop of flyline on the water, setting the fly down gently.

The taper can be formed by knotting several different diameters of nylon together, but the disadvantage of so doing is that the knots can impede the sinking rate of the leader and can also create a fish-disturbing wake near the fly in calm water. Also, knots are weaknesses, no matter how well tied they are, and the fewer knots in the tackle, the better it is.

Any knotless-tapered leader may be lengthened by joining additional lengths of nylon to it, either a thicker piece than the heavy butt end, or a tippet of the same diameter as the tip, or slightly thinner. I usually add to the thin end.

Knots

I do not like loops in my nylon leader butts to attach them to the tip of the flyline. They can hold bubbles of air and create fish-disturbing flash. A loop also makes a big wake. I prefer to make a small whipped loop in the flyline tip and knot the leader to that. Again, about 5 cm (2 in) of the plastic coating is removed, the core folded back to form the loop and a tight whipping is made with very fine stocking repair thread, to keep the two ends together. A drop of Super Glue 3 holds all secure. This system permits quick changes of leader, if necessary. The knot is simply cut near the flyline loop and another leader

Having a Hardy Troutfisher
net on a ring fixed to a
leather shoulder-strap,
keeps it out of the way but
instantly accessible.

knotted on. The loop I form is only big enough to permit me to thread the nylon leader through, about 3 mm ($\frac{1}{8}$ in) across.

Some fishermen like to attach the leader to the flyline with a whipping knot, called a needle or nail knot. This is very easy to do without a nail or needle. Holding the flyline tip in one hand, and the leader butt overlapping it by about 20 cm (8 in), wind the leader five times round the flyline and bring the end of the leader back in a loop so that the butt end faces up the flyline. Hold everything firmly between finger and thumb and use the upper side of the loop of nylon to form a whipping knot; the original twists you formed round the tip of the flyline will untwist as you progress. When all the twists have been removed, pull on the tag end and the main part of the leader, gently at first, snugging down the turns of nylon with finger and thumb so that they butt up tightly against each other about 3 mm ($\frac{1}{8}$ in) from the tip of the flyline. Pull tight, snip off the tag end and the knot is complete.

Perfectionists often push the leader into the end of the line and out of the side before making the knot, but there is no real advantage in so doing.

Apart from the whipping knot, or nail/needle knot, I recommend the use of only three other knots in nylon for flyfishing purposes: the Cove or four-turn water knot for adding tippet material to the leader in nylon of 2.7 kg (6 lb) test and under; the blood knot for joining heavy nylon – 6.8–9 kg (15–20 lb) test – to extend the thick butt of the leader; and the grinner knot for attaching the fly to the tippet. No other knots are necessary to know and these three are the best for their various tasks. All four knots are illustrated on pages 167–169. The tag end of the Cove knot may be used to attach a dropper fly, using the end that projects up the leader towards the thicker butt section. By so doing, the dropper fly is kept away from the main leader by its angle and pressure of the water as the fly is fished back.

Accessories

Still-water flyfishing demands a number of accessories. A reliable landing net is essential and the best for bank fishing is a lightweight but strong alloy net with a round or pear-shaped frame that swivels down to lie alongside the handle. It should be of the extending type and have a strong clip to attach to a round brass or stainless steel ring sewn to a 12 mm ($\frac{1}{2}$ in) leather strap worn over the shoulder. The net then hangs down at one's lower back, out of the way, but can be quickly pulled round by the strap and unclipped to land a fish. This is much better than having the net clipped to a ring on a fishing waistcoat under one's free arm – not the rod arm, where it does get in the way. Also, when fishing in wet weather, it is a simple matter to put on a waterproof jacket and sling the net over the top of it, instead of having it beneath the coat on the waistcoat ring, and inaccessible.

For boat fishing, a rigid round frame on a strong handle at least 1.8 m (6 ft) long is best. Net frames for bank and boat fishing need be no more than 55 cm (22 in) across, provided the bag-shaped net is at least 60 cm (2 ft) deep. I have landed 3.1 kg (7 lb) trout easily in a 50 cm (20 in) frame with a net of that depth. It is capable of engulfing fish up to 4.5 kg (10 lb).

Mobility is essential in bank fishing, which is why I do not recommend a wading net with a spike on it, to be stuck into the bank or lake bed when fishing. It is easy to leave it there in the excitement of following a rising fish along the bank, and then have no way of landing the fish should you hook it. Some fishermen say they see no use for a net and drag their fish on to the bank, but that cannot be done when using delicate leaders, nor can it be done when wading among marginal weeds that may stretch 6 m (20 ft) or more out into the water.

Again for reasons of mobility and comfort on the bank, a fishing waistcoat, rather than a haversack, is a necessity, in which to carry gear and food, etc. The multi-pocketed waistcoat distributes the weight of all the gear it holds evenly from both shoulders, with a place for everything and everything in its place. The best I have found is made from gaberdine and has eighteen pockets, some inside, some out, including a vast cargo pouch across the outside lower back, but accessible with the left hand, that carries a lightweight waterproof parka, some food and drink, and other larger items.

The items I find it necessary to carry in my waistcoat for every trip – they remain in there, so that I simply have to grab the waistcoat from its coat-hanger in the tackle cupboard of my den and can go fishing at a few minutes notice – include the following: four flyboxes containing dry flies, nymphs, traditional wet flies and lures, and leaded nymphs; four spools of nylon for tippets – 900 g, 1.3 kg, 1.8 kg, 2.2 kg (2 lb, 3 lb, 4 lb and 5 lb); a small priest for killing fish humanely before removing the fly; a thermometer for taking water temperatures; half a dozen spare knotless-tapered leaders; a tin of 'Gink' fly and leader/line flotant; a plastic tub of Fullers earth mixed with detergent liquid, for sinking leaders; a pair of Hardys' scissor-pliers, for cutting nylon and removing hooks – these are worn clipped to the outside left breast on a little gadget that has a retracting lanyard controlled by a coiled spring; two reels with two spare spools; a stringer on which to carry my fish without getting slime all over the place; a small square of car inner-tube rubber, which will straighten kinked leaders when they are pulled slowly but firmly through it when it is folded over; polarized spectacles, which enable me to watch my fly, or leader, or line in a ripple on sunny days without eye strain, and also permit me to see fish flash as they feed under water; a wader-repair outfit in a little box; a piece of cloth for keeping my hands clean and dry; a marrow-spoon, for pushing down a freshly killed trout's throat to discover its latest diet; a small plastic screw-top jar to take home any unusual fly specimens for closer examination; a roll of plastic adhesive tape – for emergency repairs of all kinds; a piece of wax candle for treating rod spigots; a waterproof tube containing red-top matches; a tube of insect repellent and another of ointment for treating their bites when the repellent does not do its job; a Swiss Army pocket knife and a small wedge of fine Arkansas stone for sharpening hooks.

The waterproof jacket goes into the back pocket when I leave the car should the weather look like rain. Worn over a shirt and sometimes with a sweater, the waistcoat keeps me warm and comfortable, and will afford sufficient protection from most light showers without the need for the waterproof parka.

For boat fishing, which needs better weather protection, and where mobility is not required, a large haversack will carry all the gear required, plus a waterproof hooded parka and overtrousers, since thighboots are unnecessary in a boat, wellington boots or similar being adequate.

Boat fishing

Boat fishing, besides requiring a longer, lissom rod, a long-handled landing net and maybe more lures – on reservoirs at any rate – than the bank fisher needs, also demands other accessories for maximum enjoyment. A cushion to sit on is very important, and since most boat thwarts are so low that, when sitting and fishing, one's knees are under one's chin, many boat specialists carry a long board which they rest across the gunwales of the boat, so that they can sit comfortably in a high position.

A drogue – which is a kind of sea-anchor that slows the drift of a boat in wind – is also necessary. The best is made of nylon, is light, packs into a tiny roll for carrying, and dries quickly.

It is also best to carry one's own anchor – a proper one with flukes and at least 1.2 m (4 ft) of chain between its ring and the 45.7 m (50 yd) of nylon rope that is sometimes necessary to hold the boat still over deep water in a wind.

Some boat flyfishing experts carry special rudders which they clamp to hired boats for controlling the direction of the boat's drift, but on many waters such devices are banned, mainly because clamps damage boats if carelessly used. In any case, carrying everything the boat fisher is likely to need seems rather ridiculous to me; some of these men carry mountains of such gear and it can take them half an hour to get it all into the boat and fitted up from wherever the car is parked!

There are one or two other little accessories that are sometimes useful to the still-water flyfisher, but I will deal with these when discussing the kinds of conditions in which they are beneficial.

Casting

Anybody who expects me to discuss casting in these pages is going to be disappointed. Casting cannot be learnt from a book, whether there are elaborate stroboscopic photographs with the advice or not. Casting can be learnt only from another good caster who has the ability to pass on his knowledge, and I would advise any beginner to spend money on a few lessons with a good professional instructor before ever putting line to water. Trying to learn to cast when one has paid for a day's fishing is rather like getting a good seat at the Cup Final, and then reading a paper while the game is on!

I'll say only a few words here that seem to me to be most important. Technique is what counts, not brute force. Grip the rod handle comfortably, not too tightly, with the thumb on top and facing straight up the rod, or with thumb and forefingers forming a cradle, or, for short-range delicate and accurate casts *with a light outfit*, with the forefinger extended up the handle and directly on top – that is, opposite the direction in which the reel faces. The thumb-up is perhaps best, but if it is not comfortable for you, try another grip.

The backward and forward normal overhead cast should begin slowly and end faster, with a conscious flick to speed up the rod tip and line. The forward cast should be rather like holding a hammer and knocking a nail in a wooden wall directly in front of your shoulder. Always ensure the reel faces directly

The thumb-on-top grip is a good one and should be adopted if found comfortable. The rod is a Diamondback 2.5 m (8½ ft) 3–5; the reel a Hardy Marquis 6, paint removed and alloy polished.

Some find the divided grip better and it works quite well, although it is more difficult to stop the rod drifting too far back.

Right: Keep the reel facing in the direction of the cast. That way the wrist's peak driving force can be used, as when hammering.

Far right: Let the wrist and reel do this, and the wrist has little power to produce good casting technique. It is one of the most common errors of style.

to the front, with the wrist straight, the hand held as if you were going to punch somebody; the worst mistake of all is to allow the wrist (in a right-handed caster) to bend with the reel facing away to the right. Try knocking a nail in with the wrist bent thus, and you will see that no power can be applied in that way.

Finally, ensure that the loop of line you cast in the air is formed vertically, so that the line travels and turns over directly over the tip of the rod, which should be almost perpendicular, perhaps with a slight bias to the right on the backward movement, which will prevent the line, and the fly, catching on each other due to following *exactly* the same path in both directions.

I recommend that the right-handed caster uses his reel with the handle to the left, winding being done with the left hand, which avoids changing hands to play a fish.

Chapter Four

Going fishing: the season on still water

Trout fishing seasons open at that time called spring; in the northern hemisphere any time between early March and May, in September or October in the southern hemisphere. In high mountain country, lakes may still be ice-rimmed in late May. Many a 1 April opening day – a popular general date in the British Isles – has been graced with snow and sleet; others have seen blazing sunshine and temperatures in the low 20°s C (70°s F).

So, spring, for the trout fisherman, is the time of a new beginning, when the flies he dressed throughout the long winter months will be tested with wonderful anticipation. The weather on the lake, pond or reservoir may be icy or warm, but the only important matter is the condition of the trout themselves, and, to a large extent, that depends not on the immediate weather pattern but the overall weather of the winter, between November and March.

A relatively mild winter will mean water temperatures in which trout may feed, although little growth may be shown. On many a 1 April, brown trout in fine condition may be caught; on just as many first days, browns will be lean and still showing the ravages of spawning four or five months before.

Rainbows, being a mixed race now in many parts of Britain, may be in full spawning livery in April, the cocks with big hooked jaws and livid flanks, the hens dull and spilling ripe orange eggs. Both are likely to be slimy and soft to the touch. Yet on the same day as fish in this condition are caught, some rainbows in good shape will be taken, fish that may have got rid of eggs the previous autumn, or reabsorbed them – bright silver fish that fight hard and have pink flesh.

That, then, is the early-season situation facing the still-water flyfisher. In natural lakes containing only browns, especially those with good spawning streams, April fishing can be very good. On reservoirs stocked only with rainbows, the fisherman may have to roam the water until he finds pockets of fish that are in good condition, or fails to do so, as the case may be. In waters holding both browns and rainbows, the fisherman has to take what comes, although even in that situation there are ways of avoiding the poor-conditioned trout.

When opening the season on any still water between mid-March, which is too early, and 1 May, which is usually a reasonable first day, both species of

Opposite: Crouching to keep a low profile, the fisherman casts to trout feeding beneath the willows along this lovely little Hampshire chalk-stream, the Wallop Brook, a tributary of the famous Test.

trout will usually be swimming or lying deep in the water. But deep is a relative term; many fishermen think it is necessary to find water 9 m (30 ft) deep and fish the fly 7.6 m (25 ft) down at any time before the middle of May, but my experience has been that deep water often holds the spawny rainbows and the lean, non-feeding browns at such times. I like to find water off the bank that is at least 2.4 m (8 ft) deep within casting range, and begin fishing my fly about 30 cm (1 ft) off the bottom, fishing slowly and methodically with a leaded fly that imitates one or other of the creatures that may be expected to be moving around at that time; a caddis imitation, perhaps, since early trout so often come to net with their stomachs packed with them, or a shrimp, or some kind of beetle.

So early season still-water trouting is usually best done at depth, but not always. A damp, warm day may see a few trout rising in the early afternoon, usually to small black midges hatching out. And often, too, a fly fished 90 cm (1 yd) down in water 1.8 m (6 ft) or so deep will produce nice fish, whereas the fishermen concentrating on getting down 6 m (20 ft) or so into the depths, with sunken lines and big, dark-hued lures may be catching plenty of fish, but most of them spawny rainbows or lean browns.

I used to ponder the reason for this phenomenon, which is a fairly common one, and the theory I arrived at is this: the spawny rainbows are in the depths of the deeps because the water is warmer there – spawning fish seldom feed very heavily, if at all – and they do not like very cold water. Rainbows that spawned in autumn are hungry and need to build themselves up, and so they are to be found where the bulk of the food creatures are – in the shallower, weedy water. The lean browns in the deeps may have spawned with the autumn-spawning rainbows, or tried to, and are still sickly. The browns that did not spawn at all, or did so successfully (that is, got rid of eggs or milt, or reabsorbed ova) are, like the rainbows, looking for food to get back into condition again.

I am fully aware that there are holes in that theory, but the fact remains that the fish I catch, fishing imitatively in the reasonably shallow margins, are nearly always in fair-to-good condition while the fishermen using lures on sunk lines in the depths usually catch more trout, but most of them are in spawny or poor condition.

Why should spawny rainbows, the cock fish especially, attack a deep-fished lure when they are not keen on feeding? The answer, I think, is one of territorial imperative: the big lure is seen at eyeball level as an intruder in the mating scene and the trout seeks to drive it away in the only way he knows how – by biting it.

But enough of theory: come fishing with me on an early April day, on a reservoir.

Spring

Since spring days can be rather windy I will use a 2.60 m (8½ ft) graphite rod and a double-taper size 6 floating line to begin with. That combination is reasonably delicate – fish are not likely to be too wary of fishing activity and lines at this time of the year, anyway – and has the muscle to cast into a breeze quite well. Because prevailing winds at that season are often from the south-

Left: Wild brown trout
from mountain and moor-
land rivers are usually
highly coloured, like this
little beauty from the upper
Conway in North Wales, or
are dark, with rich, red
spots.

Below left: The author on
Ireland's beautiful Blackwater in summer. These
two fish took a size 10 low
water fly from the same
pool, and there were two
other fine fish in the bag at
the end of the day.

west, I would choose the north shore, provided the wind is not too strong,
since waves create a food larder on the lee shore. Bays and headlands often
provide ideal places from which to fish, so that one is casting slightly with and
across the wind. If the wind were off the north shore I would still happily fish
there using my methods. It is not the immediate wind that is important,
remember, but the one that has prevailed for weeks, or at least days.

A 4.8 m (16 ft) knotless tapered leader goes on the end of my line and to the
2.2 kg (5 lb) tippet I will tie 90 cm (1 yd) of 1.8 kg (4 lb), if the rules permit.
First choice of fly will be a Stickfly, or something similar, on a long-shank
size 12 or 10 hook. The hook will have been weighted with lead wire, foil or
copper wire before the body dressing was applied, to make the fly sink more
quickly and remain at depth when being fished back.

In spring, water levels are usually high and the places I like best to fish are
where the water has flooded areas of low bushes, brush, long grasses or hedge-
rows leading into the water. Insects, shrimps and beetles like to crawl up
stems and branches, which also afford them shelter, and trout find their
movements above bottom, as well as on it, very attractive.

All the gear is in the fishing waistcoat, collapsible net over the back, and I
am ready to wander at will along the bank, trying the likely spots. First,
though, the leader must be wiped down and straightened in the flap of rubber
inner tube. The wiping down is done with Fuller's earth and washing-up liquid,
mixed to a paste, which lets the nylon sink quickly. A quick touch with the
Arkansas stone on the hook point and it's time to start.

At this stage, most anglers will wade straight into the water and begin
casting their utmost from a thigh-deep position. They know why they should
not, but they still do it. If they could only see the numbers of trout shooting
away from the margin as they wade in!

The line is pulled out through the tip ring so there is some 1.8 m (6 ft)
hanging, the leader is held in the left hand and the rod moved quickly back
and forth, getting line and leader into the air. More line is stripped from the
reel and follows the other until some 9 m (10 yd) is rolling back and forth,
then, with feet still on dry land, the fly is set down on the water, angling
slightly downwind.

Even a leaded long-shank fly takes a long time to sink to 2.1–2.4 m (7–8 ft):
in still air and calm water, maybe half a minute, and longer if the line is pulled
round in a bow by wind or surface drift. I usually wait until the whole leader
has disappeared before I begin recovering line, either in a figure-eight movement or by slow draws with the left hand, the line held against the rod handle
with the right hand forefinger. The former method is best if the bank is brush-
covered, since dropping recovered line among vegetation invites tangles on
the next cast. A line-holder strapped around the hips and worn on the left
thigh – for a right-handed caster – will prevent the problem, recovered line
being dropped into that.

Fish really slowly, keeping an eye rivetted on the tip of the fluorescent line
for a sudden jerk, or round-the-bend movement, or a stoppage in the line's
drift downwind. All may be a fish taking the fly and all should be struck
quickly but without a great heave, the rod moving upwards and away from the

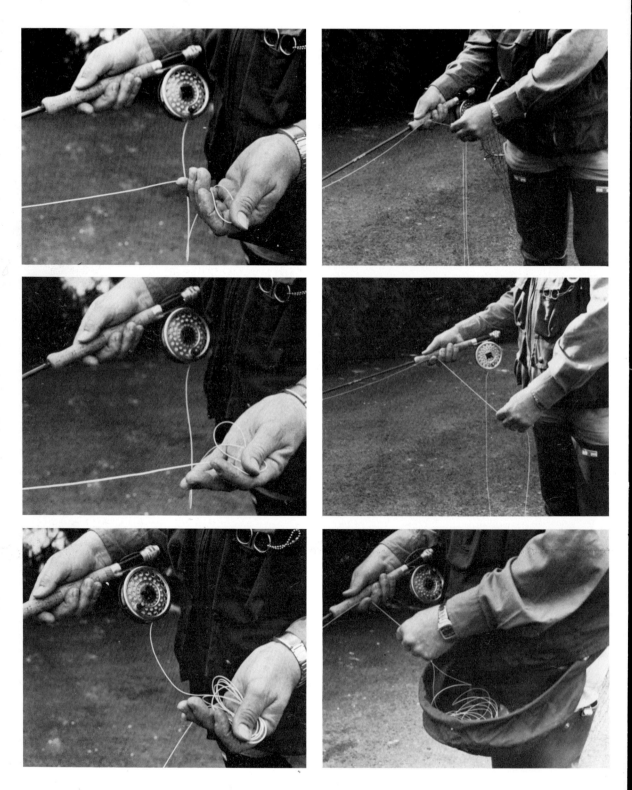

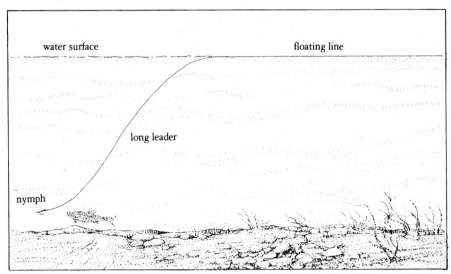

water surface   floating line

long leader

nymph

Deep nymph fishing in
still water

line's direction, left hand pulling as well (when figure-eighting) or forefinger
clamping the line against the cork.

The idea is to sink the hook point in the trout's jaw before it registers the
deception and ejects the fly. Too many anglers wait until they *feel* a pull on the
line before lifting into the fish, and quite often, when fishing a nymph deep
and slowly, they simply feel a quick tug and the fish is off. One has to appreciate
the amount of slack to be taken up in the line, floating, and the sunken leader
going down at an angle to the fly.

In a big ripple, or in difficult light conditions, it may be impossible to see
the tip of the line at a range of 18.3 m (20 yd) or more, in which case there is
no alternative but to await a tactile pull – but fish will be lost due to shallow
hooking. At the same time, when fishing very slowly, to simulate the caddis
or Alder-fly larva, or beetle, shrimp or spider crawling slowly in little hesitant
sorties across the bottom, or over submerged weeds, grass or brush, trout
feeding heavily on creatures well imitated by your artificial may be totally
fooled and will actually swallow the fly instead of spitting it out again when
the deception registers. That is very satisfying, because it means your efforts
at deception have been totally successful.

The margins may produce a fish, then, or they may not. Once some 18.3 m
(20 yd) or so of line have covered the water, with feet still on dry land, then,
and only then, begin to wade slowly and quietly into the water. Fish the spot
for half an hour, whether fish have been taken or not, trying the fly just
touching bottom up to about midwater. If the Stickfly does not work, then
try a Black and Peacock Spider (leaded) or a size 10 Pheasant Tail Nymph
(leaded) with a thorax of natural wild rabbit fur.

If these fail too, move to another spot and try all over again. Fishing the
deep nymph like this when no fish are visible on the surface demands considerable concentration. In sunlight on ripple, wear polarizing glasses to
avoid eye-strain when watching the line for takes. Vary the retrieve, too. The
very slow, even recovery usually works best early in the season, but a series

Far left, top to bottom: The
figure-eight method of
recovering line; the coils of
line are picked up by the
little finger and held by the
thumb and forefinger.

Left, top and middle: The
stripping method of line
recovery, which may be
used to move the fly fast or
very, very slowly.

Left, bottom: Stripping line
into a line-holder. This
keeps line out of the water,
vegetation on the bank, and
prevents wind causing
tangles, and blowing it
away on the water.

of short, sharp jerks followed by a pause, then a long, slow pull on the line, will sometimes move lethargic fish. Trout in cold 'early-season' water are less likely to chase after a fly than in the 18°C (65°F) of midsummer.

It is obviously an advantage to know the lake or reservoir being fished, so that deep ditches, pockets of weed and other features hidden by the high water of spring can be located and investigated. Small, sheltered bays are often very productive in early spring, and quite often a rise will begin in such places after mid-day when no surface activity is visible in the open water, simply because the water in the bay is a little warmer and so encourages insects (midges) to hatch.

Should the wind be strong enough, from one side or the other, to drag the floating flyline and the sunk fly too quickly, thus lifting the fly in the water, the action may be slowed down by changing from a floating line to a sink-tip line. The sunken line tip acts as a brake in the water, and the fly will fish round more slowly and thus at a greater depth.

In very strong wind, it may even be necessary to fish with a slow-sinking line that still permits a slow recovery, in which case a weight-forward line will be best. Of course, the takes must then be detected by touch, and again, some fish will undoubtedly be missed, or played briefly before being lost,

Concentration on the floating leader or line tip is essential when nymph fishing in calm conditions. The author figure-eights and uses polarizing glasses to reduce glare.

simply because they detected the fraud, or the hook only obtained a tiny hold in the skin of the jaw and they broke free.

Should the afternoon turn warm, with a few fish taking hatching flies from the surface, it is great fun to fish for them. Fishing for visible trout is far more interesting than searching the depths. If fish are seen to be taking insects at the surface in April, it is most likely they are taking a small Black Midge pupa or an Orange/Silver Midge pupa, both species hatching in that month.

Actually, if you have the confidence to do so, it often pays to try fishing an imitation of one or other of these midge pupae – size 12 is a useful one to start with – within 60 cm (2 ft) of the surface if the deep, leaded-nymph technique has failed to produce. Quite often on a cold April day I have tried this near-surface midge pupa technique and have taken fish that gave firm takes and were later found to be feeding on midge pupae. And I have done so when there had been no signs of surface activity at all.

Some flyfishers never do manage to become successful using slow-fished imitations, whether deep down or on the surface, and for them the technique of the lure is the natural progression, although I tend to think of it as a retrograde step. Some who do not succeed give up too early in their apprenticeship. Others simply do not have the good sight necessary to see leader or line movements at any great distance.

Lure fishing, from the bank or a boat, demands a stiffer rod, heavier line and stronger, shorter leader than is used for fishing imitatively in early season. Successful lures are usually dressed on long-shank hooks, size 8, 6 or even 4, and flies of this size and bulk demand a heavy line to push and pull them through the air. A weight-forward or shooting-taper, size 8, will cast such lures 27.4 or 36.5 m (30–40 yd) or more respectively, and fish them deeply if the line is a fast-sinking type. Some lure fishers use size 9 and 10 sinking shooting-tapers, but that is taking a hammer to crack a nut. The only times these size 9 and 10 lines are necessary is when using a very bulky fly, such as a size 4 Muddler or a tandem up to 10 cm (4 in) in length, for very big predatory trout, or when fishing very deep – 6 m (20 ft) or more down – from a boat in hot summer weather, when a fast-sinking heavy line is needed to get the fly down to fishing depth quickly, and keep it there while it is being fished back.

A size 8 long-shank lure usually needs a 2.7 kg (6 lb) tippet, to have the stiffness to turn the fly over in the air and to absorb the sudden shock of a fish grabbing the fly while the line is being stripped back in. That is not to say that the line is being, or needs to be stripped back very fast, as many lure fishers may be seen to do. However, even a long, slow pull in one direction, coinciding with a sudden pull in the opposite direction can impose great strain on the leader. Many lure fishers use 4.5 kg (10 lb) tippets when fishing lures 7.5 cm (3 in) long or more for big trout.

There are many lure patterns, in which, for simplicity, I am including such flies as streamers and bucktails, dressed with whole hackle wings and bunched hair wings respectively. They come in gaudy colours with flashy tinsel bodies or ribbings, and in dull hues – brown, black or plain white. However, a basically black or basically white lure will work most of the time, and when neither does, then an orange one should do the trick.

Early season trout appear to take black lures best – patterns like Black Lure, Black Marabou, Sweeney Todd. The black will also catch fish in summer, but often white does well on an evening when darkness comes sooner than it should. In bright summer weather, an orange fly can be deadly. White Marabou or Bob Church's Appetiser are both good; the orange range is well represented by such patterns as Whisky and Price's Orange Streamer.

A rod of 2.75–2.90 m (9–9½ ft) for the size 8 line will carry the big, air-resistant fly well clear of one's head on the forward cast, and has the stiffness to punch it out a long way, even into a wind. When lure fishing at depths of 4.5 m (15 ft) or more, a long cast – at least 22.8 m (25 yd), and better, 37 m (40 yd) – is necessary so that the fly fishes at depth for as long a distance as possible before the angle of the line to the rod tip beings to pull it to the surface again.

Since long casting with heavy weight-forward lines and shooting tapers causes considerable surface disturbance, it is best, in general, to select deep water close to the bank, and water with wind on it to produce a ripple. Ripple camouflages disturbance from the fish.

The basics of lure fishing from the bank are fairly simple: cast as far as possible, allow the lure and line time to sink to a point close to the bottom and to midwater (in April and May, anyway) and then fish it back in long, slow pulls, trying to achieve a smooth progress of the lure through the water. It pays to count in seconds as the line sinks, and to remember the count-down time so that a successful fishing depth, once found, may be attained consistently.

Point the rod straight down the line when retrieving, but when that sudden lunging pull comes, do not make an opposing yank. Instead, lift the rod

The author's son plays a lively rainbow from a boat on ultra-light graphite rod and size 3 line.

smoothly, gripping the line against the cork handle of the rod, but yield line a little if the pull becomes excessive. Often lure-caught trout hook themselves by taking the lure hard and then turning away, but quite as often the hook-hold is only skin-deep and a firm pull is needed to sink the barb.

Deep water off dam faces, when fishing from them is permitted on reservoirs, is good for early season lure fishing at depth. To find deep water from the bank, examine the lie of the land and fish those areas where the land slopes steeply down into the water.

Since so much thin running line (with a weight-forward line) or shooting line (with a shooting-taper) will be dropped while recovering the lure, it is necessary to use a line receptacle when bank fishing. Few waters have banks that are snag-free enough to make it practical to drop recovered line on the bank or in the shallow margin. The thin line will surely be snagged and ruin the forward cast. Also, when wading, the recovered line tends to sink and tangle if dropped into the water – and sunken shooting line will not shoot freely. The line tray low on the line-hand thigh is a good idea.

Early-season boat fishing on reservoirs and lakes, which includes the big natural Scottish and Irish ones, is usually done with sinking lines, too. The boat is either anchored over suitable water and the anglers fish downwind or down and across, or it is allowed to drift as slowly as possible with the wind, its progress slowed by a drogue, which is an underwater parachute on a cord. Some reservoir fishermen use a collapsible rudder, which is fixed to the transom and used to steer the drifting boat at a fixed distance from the bank, following its outline into bays and round headlands.

On the big natural lakes, teams of traditional wet flies, winged and hackled patterns, are popular, and they are usually fished 80–90 cm (2–3 ft) down, on the drift, no matter what the water depth. Brown trout in natural lakes are more likely to be feeding in cold surface water than stocked rainbows, and the method can be quite effective.

On reservoirs, however, the use of sinking shooting-tapers joins that of traditional flyfishing on the drift, and the big lures are fished as described from the bank. Wherever possible, though, experienced reservoir boat fishers will anchor over deep water, close to the dam face or where there are drop-offs or trenches in the lake bed, to get their lines and lures down deep and fish them back slowly. In cold water trout are not inclined to chase after their food as they are in the warmer temperatures of late spring and summer.

Cold weather conditions in Britain, and elsewhere, often continue well into May, and the cold-water tactics referred to here will still be useful at such times. However, in a mild spring, when May water temperatures in the margins and surface levels of still waters are around 13°C (55°F), aquatic life begins to stir, although it is usually early June before trout begin to form a regular pattern of surface feeding in the early mornings and in the evenings, generally from about an hour before sunset. Really good rises generally occur when the water temperature is steady at 15–21°C (60–70°F), after which the water is usually too warm for fish to be comfortable and therefore actively feeding.

It has often been said that only rainbows will feed in 21°C (70°F) plus water temperatures and that browns prefer cooler water, up to about 20°C (68°F).

But having taken both browns and rainbows in fairly equal numbers on a number of different days over a period when the water temperature, taken in the area I was fishing, ranged from 20°C to 22°C (68–71°F), I now believe that the upper level of brown trout feeding activity is not so dependent purely on water temperature as we have been led to believe. Tom Ivens, the doyen of British still-water trout fishers, records catching browns and rainbows in equal numbers in 21°C (70.5°F).

In a mild spring, mid-May sees the beginning of the best trout flyfishing on still waters. Several species of midges will by then be hatching, plus upwing flies like Lake and Pond Olives, the Sepia Dun, which may hatch in a warm April, some land-bred flies that get blown on to the water, and there will be increased activity of many other forms of water life.

With water temperatures at about 11°C (52°F) minimum up to about 15°C (60°F) during this transitional period (the measurement being taken at about 60 cm/2 ft), both brown and rainbow trout are likely to have discovered that there is an increased amount of insect and other animal food in the upper levels of the water and they are likely to take a fly fished within 90 cm (1 yd) of the surface, or within 12 mm ($\frac{1}{2}$ in) of the surface, as the case may be. As always, experimentation in fishing depth and speed is the key to success.

From this point in the season onwards, try to remember that trout will want to be feeding as much as they are able. They are voracious, if sometimes delicate feeders, and unless the water is very cold indeed (below 9°C/48°F) or above about 21°C (70°F) the fish will always be where the food is.

However, other factors govern trout behaviour as well as the need to eat. Some need not concern us, since we cannot know too much about them from the immediate signs: oxygen content of the water is one example. Strong sunlight on a calm lake with clear water is not conducive to surface feeding, since they have no eyelids to reduce the amount of light on their eyes. They go deeper or seek shade. In a ripple, however, the light is scattered and fish will swim near the surface at such times.

Look for signs of rising fish. It is the prime aim of any fisherman to locate his quarry before commencing to fish: it is futile to try to catch fish where there are none, yet many do just this, more often than not. Rings, vees on the surface, splashes, are all signs of surface or subsurface feeding; by subsurface I mean within 15 cm (6 in). Remember, however, that an absence of visible surface signs of trout feeding does not mean that there are no fish feeding just subsurface either. A trout can take a fly or nymph, or whatever, 15 cm (6 in) down and give no sign. This type of feeding is usually done in a leisurely manner, when there is plenty of food about; a fish moving quickly to snatch a morsel 15 cm (6 in) or more below the surface will nearly always make some disturbance on the surface. In calm water, this may be a tiny ring, or a whirl-pool-like formation; in a ripple, the movement may simply cause a slight flattening or calm area to appear suddenly.

So there is no way of knowing if trout are feeding subsurface where no signs show, except by test-fishing.

With the warmer conditions and more food available, more trout will now be inclined to swim into the marginal shallows, maybe into water 90 cm

Emergent vegetation in the margins often holds big browns that move in to feed at first and last light. The author wades out to await the twilight witching hour.

(3 ft) deep. Later in the summer, even 30 cm (1 ft) of water, especially over flooded grass, bushes or weedbeds, is deep enough for fish to venture into.

Because the fly will now be offered to trout seen rising or patrolling a stretch of water, delicacy of presentation is that much more important. Fish near the surface are always more wary than those lying deeper; they have an inbuilt fear of predatory birds and other fish-eating creatures, and a mere shadow appearing nearby, or a splash, will send them diving for safety.

For bank work I choose a lightweight graphite rod, between 2.45–2.70 m (8–8¾ ft) long, and a size 3–4 double-taper floating line, coloured fluorescent orange for visibility. The knotless-tapered leader, 4.8–7.6 m (16–25 ft) long, will have a tippet of 1.3–2.2 kg (3–6 lb) test; if the fishery rules do not permit tippets below 2.2 kg (5 lb) test, as some state, choose an extra-strong, thin nylon, like Platil Strong, which gives strength with slimness. In 2.5 kg (5½ lb) test this nylon is thinner than ordinary nylon 700 g (1½ lb) weaker.

If fish are rising within reach, obviously I will fish for them. My first choice of fly would be something to imitate a hatching midge pupa of a size and colour likely to be about: a size 12 or 14 black one, or maybe an orange/silver or a pale green. If these failed to work, I would switch to a size 12 Pheasant Tail Nymph; I might, in fact, have begun with the PTN, which is perhaps the most useful imitative fly pattern, representing a wide selection of natural insects, available to the flyfisher.

I like to fish close to the surface first, and this will happen naturally for the first few casts, since the leader and fly – unleaded – are dry. When they absorb water they will penetrate the surface much more quickly. It is as well to remember, though, that even when fly and nylon have become thoroughly wetted, the fly will not fish very deeply, no matter how long it is allowed to sink for, nor how slowly it is fished. To fish a fly on a floating line at much more than 1.2–1.8 m (4–6 ft) deep, even in calm, windless conditions, a leaded fly is needed. Too many fishermen think they are fishing deep when they are not: estimates of the fly being 3.6 m (12 ft) down can usually be reduced by half.

If a fish is seen to rise, cast the fly quickly but gently to the rise, or just on the upwind side if there is a breeze, since fish mainly swim into the wind (surface current). Wait a second or two for the fly to go under, together with several centimetres of the tippet, then move the fly slowly, either by stripping or figure-eight retrieve. Watch the point where the leader submerges or, if you cannot see it, the tip of the line. Most flyline makers advise against using any flotants, since many will damage polyvinyl chloride, but because it is absolutely essential that your line floats high on the surface, specially the slim tip, it should be thinly smeared with a flotant that will not harm it (such as 'Gherke's Gink' or 'Sue Burgess Fly Flotant').

If the fish boils near where you think your fly is, quickly lift the rod to tighten the line. If you see the floating part of the leader jerk forward or move in any unusual manner, also tighten. If the line tip does the same, again tighten. Too many fishermen wait until they feel a pull before tightening, and often lose fish or miss them completely.

This visual fishing takes a great deal of concentration and practice, but once it is mastered it will catch you many more fish than your companions using the tactile method. Of course, you will sometimes get a fast take that is felt before it is seen – more likely, simultaneously – but I have watched hundreds of fishermen get takes to which they never reacted at all, because they never realized that a fish had accepted their sunken fly.

Mid-May normally sees the beginning of that delightful phenomenon, the evening rise, which may begin as early as 7.30 pm or as late as 8.45 pm, which leaves very little time to fish before darkness falls. Again, the midges are nearly always responsible for the rise at this time of the year, since they tend to move towards the surface as the light goes, to hatch. Daytime fishing from this time until well into July will nearly always produce fish, some of which may be seen rising.

It takes confidence to fish a single nymph slowly near the surface where no trout are seen moving, but very often fish will be taken that way. Try to believe that every cast you make, and every retrieve, is going to produce a take. Confidence seems to make fish take; probably something to do with the way the fly is fished by the confident fisherman. It may seem a strange claim to make, but

There *is* more to flyfishing than catching fish. Nick Cranfield's camera catches the author fishing on Rutland Water's Hambleton Peninsula.

at times when I am fishing really well and catching fish at fairly regular intervals, I can sense a take a split second before it actually occurs and others have told me of similar experiences.

When fish are feeding within 2.5 cm (1 in) of the surface, even 12 mm ($\frac{1}{2}$ in), make sure that you fish your fly no deeper. Use flotant on your leader to within about 2.5 cm (1 in) of the fly to do so. Fish extra slowly, since any drag from where the leader submerges to the fly will cause a minute wake. If your fly is 7.5 cm (3 in) down when fish are swimming subsurface, taking midge pupae hanging from the surface film preparatory to hatching, the trout will never see your fly because the eye of the fish will be, maybe, 2.5 cm (1 in) from the surface and looking up. I stress again: fishing depth is critical.

When the fly fished down to about 1.5 m (5 ft) produces no takes, and you have tried several different patterns and different speeds and types of recovery, then it may well be that the fish are feeding nearer the bottom, if they are in the area at all. Try the leader nymph for a while, as for the early April style; it often works.

Having tried subsurface and deep fishing without an offer, move to another area. If there is a breeze at all, I like to have it blowing along and off my bank.

A final word about the evening rise, which applies to such times later in the season too. The rise may often last for only ten or fifteen minutes before the fish stop feeding or go down and out to deeper water. It is essential to be quick to take advantage of this hectic feeding period, since there are days when fishing before and after this brief rise will produce only the odd fish, or none at all.

Do not wade in and out of the water to land and kill your fish. Having landed (netted) a trout, kill it quickly with the priest where you stand. Remove the fly, then string the fish on your stringer, attached to your belt, or leave it in the net hanging over your shoulder. Cast again as quickly as possible. This way, you maximize your fishing time and do not cause disturbance by wading to and from the bank. This is why the fishing waistcoat containing all your tackle needs is such an advantage. A bag on the bank is useless.

So far I have written only about using a single fly on the leader, and this is intentional because experience has shown that only occasionally is a dropper of great benefit. Droppers can tangle in the net when netting a fish, thereby losing it; or the other fly, being towed around among underwater vegetation by a hooked fish, will often snag and the fish will break free or come unhooked.

However, when I cannot easily discover what colour midge pupa, or other fly the fish are taking, I sometimes cut down the experimenting period by using two flies of different colours or sizes. I rarely have the dropper more than 1.8 m (6 ft) from the point fly and I tie that 1.8 m (6 ft) of nylon to the end of my knotless taper with a four-turn water knot, using the upper tag-end for the dropper fly.

Droppers are, however, useful for boat fishing during this mid-May on-wards period. With one or two droppers and using conventional winged or hackled wet fly patterns – like Butcher, Rogan's Golden Olive, Dunkeld, Black Pennell, Mallard and Claret, for example – the flies are fished on the drift and as they near the boat, the dropper or droppers are lifted to skim along the surface, making a little vee. This is very attractive to trout, especially in a ripple. Most takes will come within 60 cm (2 ft) of the surface and many to the dropper will be visible as the fish splashes at the fly.

Lure fishing from both bank and boat during this period will still catch fish, both deep down and near the surface, but such tactics are not much fun, when fish are feeding properly and willing to take small representations of their natural food.

From a boat, the lure can be fished on the drift or at anchor. On a breezy day, especially with the wind from the south or south-west and warm, the lee shore of the lake or reservoir is likely to be a good area. In a warm gale, a boat an-chored so that the lures or flies may be cast into the breaking waves near the bank, in discoloured water in which food collects or is washed from the bottom and the underwater vegetation by the turmoil, is often extremely pro-ductive. It is unlikely that bank fishermen will be present, since casting into a wind above force 5 is no picnic and is only practicable for excellent casters.

Summer

By the time June is well in, water temperatures will again have risen, given seasonally warm weather, to maybe a daily average of 18°C (64°F), sometimes falling a degree or so if a cool northerly wind gets up, or rising to nearly 20°C (68°F) when periods of settled sunny weather occur.

Now even more insects will appear. The many types of midge pupae will be joined by the sedges (caddis), which make their presence known in the evenings as they swarm in the margins and over the water, rising and falling in the air and scuttering their ungainly way across the water, like a swan trying to take off. Numerous land-bred and water-bred flies, plus the other food animals like shrimps, various beetles, spiders, water-lice and water-snails, join the increased species of those important midges. By early July damselfly nymphs will be numerous, too.

For the flyfisher, this is the rich time. If he only catches the odd fish during the day – which is sometimes the case for bank fishers – there is almost certainly a good chance of a limit bag in the evening and at dusk, when the midges and sedges appear in their millions. Clouds of midges may be like smoke over the margins and bankside bushes on some evenings.

In addition to the Black, Green and Orange/Silver Midges there may be the Golden Dun Midge, the Large and Small Red Midges, the Ribbed Midge and the Phantom Midge. It is the time of plenty for the trout and it can be so for the fisherman, too, if he masters the challenge that is often presented. For in addition to locating the fish and finding out the fishing depth and what fly will take them, he may also find the fish nerve-rackingly selective about the exact colour and size of imitation they want.

It is now, even more than previously, that the very light tackle comes into its own. Where permitted, leaders tapered to 700 g (1½ lb) tippets – or the nearest equivalent diameter in Platil Strong – tied to size 14 and even 16 flies, and the DT3 floating line, will score heavily. The lissom rod takes the shock of big trout surging around tethered by a fragile tippet, and now the fish are well-fed and fit, fighting twice as hard as they did in early April. They will also be more wary, especially of the bank fisher, on public waters, since they soon learn about the dangers of flylines and ripples, and vibrations from heavy footfalls.

It is also the time when the dry fly begins to take fish. And this, when the sedges are up in the evenings, can be the cream of the season's sport.

Days of gentle south-westerly breeze and clouds in a blue sky may produce fish all day, with an evening climax of activity. Both boat and bank fishermen have their chances and trout are eager to chase the boat fishers' droppers as they skim the waves. Lures, too, will still take trout, from bank and boat, and at their best they will be used to imitate sticklebacks mating in the margins, or other small fish, on which browns will feed heavily if such prey is available in good numbers. Then a fish-imitating lure, fished on a long leader and a floating line, is cast to where trout are seen chasing the little fish, and fished back in jerky, stripping style, or allowed to flutter down as it sinks slowly, like a dying, injured little fish.

A big trout making a wake as it follows a lure fished thus is an exciting prospect, and the savage rod-wrenching take can be like a sledge-hammer hitting the line.

As the light fails, trout will begin to rise. The rise will intensify until, on a

A rare sight: three rods bent in two boats as trout are played in an area of open water where boat fishermen have located a concentration of rainbows.

good, mild and fairly calm evening there are fish everywhere. The air hums with the wing-beats of millions of midges, and sedges flutter like snowflakes.

On goes the dry sedge pattern, to match the natural that seems to be most prevalent: it might be a Cinnamon Sedge, or a Welshman's Button, or a Silver Sedge, or Grousewing, or a Red Sedge, or even that mighty beast, the Great Red Sedge, which can be 2.5 cm (1 in) long. Or it could be one of many others.

The dry fly might need to be on a size 14 hook, to match the size of the smaller sedges, or a size 8 long-shank for the Great Red Sedge. It is first necessary to discover if the frenzied rise of trout is taking midge pupae gathering to hatch beneath the surface, or sedge pupae hatching out, or the hatched winged adult. This is not easy to do, because the fish may begin their feeding on one species of midge and then switch to another that becomes more numerous, or they may switch from the midge to the sedge, or vice versa.

My detective work begins when I try to see which sedge is the most numerous in the vicinity; or which midge. Midge pupae are difficult to see in the water margins and I usually fish a size 12 or 14 pupa, say a pale green one, on the point and another colour, perhaps blood-red or white, on the dropper. If neither produces a fish, I will try a special Pheasant Tail Nymph, dressed to represent a midge pupa, which suggests many of the dark-bodied midges, since its colour is a dull reddish-brown. I might even try a midge pupa on the point and a sedge pupa imitation on the dropper, usually a pale green and amber one, which will normally do the trick. I will also be trying changes in fishing depth and in speed of recovery. Sedge pupae, for example, move quite fast, but in short bursts, beneath the surface when they are hatching.

The whole plan is aimed at catching a feeding fish. Then, out comes the marrow-spoon and a small white dish or tin-lid. The throat and upper stomach contents of the freshly killed trout are extracted and mixed with a little water in the receptacle. This will usually show what the trout's most recently taken food was and one then has to establish which of them is most numerous.

It does not always work. In the few minutes it takes to catch the fish and do an examination of the recent diet, the other fish may have switched to something else. It is solving this jig-saw puzzle that makes trout flyfishing in the imitative style so exciting and absorbing.

Sometimes, when one has decided that the trout are taking one kind of winged sedge, for example, and one has a reasonably good imitation to tie on, it has then to be established if the trout want it cast ahead of them and just left to sit there, floating on the water, or moved in spurts to simulate the activity of the recently hatched fly as it tries to take off.

Surface activity does not necessarily indicate feeding on winged sedges. Often, the fish are taking only the sedge pupae as they approach the surface preparatory to hatching and will not accept a hatched, surface-borne fly.

On an evening of calm water conditions, the slightest movement of a midge pupa imitation being fished within 25 mm (1 in), or less, of the surface on a long greased leader, will make a fish-scaring wake, and at such times it is necessary to fish the pupa (or pupae if you use a dropper) absolutely without movement, other than that imparted by the surface drift of the water in which the naturals are borne.

Many flyfishers are set in their ways and will not believe that a fish will take a stationary midge pupa imitation, although the same fishermen will happily fish a stationary dry fly. I have often wondered why, as I have taken fish in this way while those who persisted in recovering their perfectly good imitations caught only the occasional fish, or nothing.

Sometimes trout will accept only the tiniest flies, dressed on size 16 hooks, in the evenings. Often this is due to a hatch of a tiny pale green-to-white fly known as 'the angler's curse'. It is in fact the tiny upwinged fly *Caenis*, and when trout become pre-occupied with feeding on the hatching hordes they can become very difficult indeed to catch.

Several dry patterns exist but I have never found them very effective, nor met anybody else who did. Better by far is the pattern to imitate the Phantom Midge Pupa, which is also taken by the fish for the nymph of the *Caenis*. The dressing, together with others I recommend, will be found in chapter 15.

Another mid-summer fishing condition that demands a rather special approach is the very hot, bright day with no clouds in the sky and the surface of the water mirror-calm. These conditions make traditional boat-fishing types blanch and seek solace at the nearest pub, or opt for a fast-sinking line and a lure out in the deeps. However, the bank angler – and the boat angler, too, if he can anchor his craft well – can still fish enjoyably and effectively.

In such conditions the fish will be feeding near the bottom at a depth of 3.6–6 m (12–20 ft), avoiding the bright light and, perhaps, the excessively warm top layer of water. The tactic involves finding a steeply sloping area of bank with the requisite depth of water at casting range, then fishing a nymph very slowly close to the bottom.

The double-taper floating line is needed, plus a knotless-tapered leader at least 6 m (20 ft) long, better still 7.6 m (25 ft), and with a tippet of about 2.2 kg (5 lb) test. The nymph itself should be about size 10 or 12 – no smaller – and sometimes size 8 is better, since the hook needs to be big enough to carry a double wrapping of lead wire or lead foil in several layers under the body dressing, which can be a Pheasant Tail Nymph or similar.

Weight is the key factor, not fly pattern; when trout are feeding near the bottom they usually collect anything that moves, including shrimps, midge larvae and pupae, caddis, damselfly nymphs and snails. They are not fussy.

Casting with such a long leader and a heavyweight fly is a problem: the technique involves an extra-long wait for the nymph to catch up with the loop of line and leader in both forward and backward casting movements, then making a smooth but powerful delivery, stopping the rod high on the power-stroke, to force the fly and leader to turn over and straighten out.

Once the use of the long leader and heavy fly no longer creates a presentation problem, he who can fish the deep, slow nymph will enjoy fascinating fishing on hot, calm days while other fishermen are moaning about the conditions. There must be peak concentration on the floating line tip, since often the line may move only a few centimetres before the fish realizes that the fly is not what it seems, and ejects it. The problem, of course, is that it takes time for any movement at the fly to travel up the long leader suspended almost at a right angle from the floating line tip, and be visible.

Without any wind-drift on the water it takes something like two minutes or more for a size 10 leaded PTN to sink 4.5 m (15 ft) or so and straighten the leader. Although takes will usually come during the first 30 cm (1 ft) or so of movement of the nymph, which will tend to rise from the bottom, just like a natural nymph or pupa does, the takes can also come at any time during the very slow recovery or, indeed, while the nymph is still sinking; 'on the drop' as fishermen say.

On many a day the fish may prove difficult to locate and to catch and only as dusk approaches is there a good chance of a fish, and such times are brief – maybe only fifteen minutes or so when the light has gone. Sometimes, during a good evening rise, fish are nearly uncatchable, for some strange reason, and the sole chance of a fish or two to take home comes when the rise has petered out and the surface shows little or no sign of life.

The technique involves fishing with a sink-tip or floating line and either a wake-making Muddler Minnow or a lure, such as a Black Marabou, White

Opposite: The epitomy of nymph-fishing concentration: the fisherman tries to keep his leader and line tip in view as the setting sun forms confusing light patterns on the water's surface. This is Bewl Bridge, about a mile from the author's home in Kent.

Marabou, or Appetiser. The Muddler is cast out as far as possible, from bank or boat, and then fished back quite slowly, at a speed just fast enough for it to make a little wake. Fish may be seen chasing the fly on the calm surface in the afterglow, but when the splash of the take comes it is folly to tighten immediately, since most fish will be missed or just pricked. Wait until the rod tip becomes heavy with the weight of the fish before lifting firmly.

The white or black lure is also cast a long way, allowed to sink for thirty seconds or so, and then fished as slowly as a nymph. For some strange reason, fish that have been refusing good imitative little flies will take these lures confidently and, when netted, will often be found to have the fly well back in the throat.

Muddler-type lures are also good fun to use on windy days when the weather is warm. They are cast across and downwind on a floating line – which for long casts can be a weight-forward or shooting-taper type – and stripped fast through the wave-tops. The disturbance they make will attract trout from deep down to attack them. It is not possible to continue with this method for long periods, since it is very tiring.

There is one other very important peak in the late summer period, and that is when Craneflies (daddy-long-legs) are about on the surrounding grassland and are blown on to the lake by the breeze. With a good imitation well anointed with flotant on a leader about 3 m (10 ft) long, it is possible to cast to rising fish, or simply to let the fly float for minutes on end until a fish comes up and sucks it down.

Craneflies are obviously succulent mouthfuls for big trout and browns, in particular, will fall for this ruse. Occasionally, it may be best to move the fly in little spurts, then let it remain still for several seconds. In general, however, a stationary fly works best, even in a flat calm. Many lakes and reservoirs yield their bigger trout to the dry Cranefly, as do the Irish limestone loughs when the Mayfly is hatching.

When fishing the dry fly, do not use a leader that is too long. The resistance of a dry fly in the air, due to its bulk and flared cock hackles, makes it more difficult to cast than a slim-bodied nymph or wet fly. For most dry fly work, a leader 2.7–3.6 m (9–12 ft) long is adequate.

Trout in high mountain lakes do not usually regain good condition until late May or June, and from then until late August is usually the best time for fishing these lonely waters. The fish, wild browns, will not be large – an average weight of 115 g (4 oz) is the norm. However, they fight like 'tame' trout three or more times their size and, because food is in short supply at those altitudes and in the acid water which characterizes them, any flies blown on to the surface are snapped up avidly.

Use the lightest rod and line available – and travel light – because the light tackle will provide maximum enjoyment of the small fish and the absence of heavy gear to carry makes climbing to these lakes, which may take several arduous hours, more bearable.

Wild browns in mountain lakes are seldom very selective about fly patterns, and I would be happy to confine my choice to three flies in sizes 12 and 14: the Pheasant Tail Nymph, leaded and unleaded, the Coch-y-Bondhu and Iron

Seatrout are wild, vigorous fighters and moments like this, when the fish leaps on the end of a long line, can tear out the hook. Grace Oglesby fishing a loch in the Outer Hebrides.

A trout is hooked on a small put-and-take fishery in the south of England, played to the net, and finally lifted out.

Blue. Alternatives to the two dry flies would be Tup's Indispensable, Grey Duster, Pheasant Tail or Beacon Beige. A light and a dark fly give alternative impressions.

Though these wild fish are not fussy about fly pattern, they are fussy about leader diameter, and 680–900 g (1½–2 lb) test tippets will catch many more fish than thicker ones.

There are always surprises when fishing these high-level waters, and from some in which the fish seldom grow heavier than 225 g (½ lb), the occasional monster of 1.3–1.8 kg (3–4 lb) will surprise the fisherman. A landing net, though seldom used, is a comforting standby in such cases.

Put-and-take fisheries

There is one other type of still-water trout fishing that has become increasingly popular: seeking those big stock rainbows in small put-and-take ponds and pools, quite often situated in somebody's big garden, or on a farm. To many, such fishing is too artificial, although those who also say it is too easy are not being fair to the normal situation.

To cast a dry fly or a leaded nymph to a rainbow weighing 4.5–9 kg (10–20 lb) or more, that can be seen cruising in the usually clear water on such fisheries is very exciting, and although some of these big, pellet-fed fish are easy to take, there are times when they are as difficult as any other fish.

I think the biggest problem is getting the nymph, which is generally more effective than the dry fly, down to the level of the fish at the right time for an eyeball confrontation. Most of these big fish go on regular patrol and it is far better to settle down quietly in one place on the fish's beat and, using polarizing spectacles, cast the nymph out and only move it when the fish gets close to it.

Frankly, the fight of these big rainbows has never impressed me, though some say they have had heroic battles. It has often been apparent that big fish are more usually lost because the fisherman was using heavy tackle and held on too hard, than because of the trout's fighting ability and sheer weight. I believe that, provided a leader of 2.2–2.7 kg (5–6 lb) test is used with a slim line and flexible rod, these big fish can be led to the net by a fisherman with 'hands' to gentle the fish to the net, more easily than by using bullying tactics. Hang on to one of these big fish in its limited area and it will thrash and plunge, putting sudden strain on hook and leader.

Chapter Five

Brown and rainbow trout in rivers

On the whole, flyfishing for trout in running water is easier than still-water fishing because, for much of the time, the flow of water helps one to present the fly attractively to the fish. Having said that – and realizing that it will raise the hackles of many die-hard river trout-fishers who feel that theirs is the true art – the flow can also make a fly very difficult to fish properly.

Feeding patterns

Fish location is much easier in rivers, since fish usually take up lies facing the flow in places where the food-stream is brought to them by the current. However, rivers vary greatly. Some may be gin-clear and smooth-flowing, such as the comparatively placid chalk-streams and limestone rivers found in the English West Country, in Yorkshire, in parts of Ireland, and Normandy, and the limestone streams of the North American continent. Others are brawling torrents, maybe 1.8 m (6 ft) in width, or 90 m (100 yd) wide, or more, cascading their roaring way down mountainsides and through wild moorland.

Watch a rising trout in a river on a late spring or summer day and its rises will often be at regular intervals and in more or less the same place. Such a fish is relatively easy to approach undetected from downstream, since its head is looking upstream, and a competent cast should place the fly upstream of the fish, to drift down and be taken.

Not all river trout feed in such an accommodating manner, however, and on many small streams, particularly on moorland, one has to make constant casts to places where one *expects* fish to be lying, often without a sign of a rise being seen.

Just as in still-water flyfishing, the dry fly, the nymph and traditional wet flies may be used, in different circumstances. The only method used on still waters that is used very little on rivers is the big lure on a sunken or floating line; but even this technique may be seen in these more enlightened times, whereas, a few years ago, such a thing would have been frowned upon. Indeed, it is still frowned upon in some locations: the chalk-streams, for example, where most of the fishing is limited, by established practice and rules, to dry fly and the upstream imitative nymph only. In wild rivers and streams, on the other hand, the dry fly and nymph are used alongside wet flies; the latter fished singly or in teams of two or three, cast across and allowed to drift down and, may-

Some of the most enjoyable trout fishing on rivers occurs on the little rocky streams running down from the hills or mountains. This is the upper Conway near Ysbyty Ifan.

be, to swing round with the current, until they are downstream of the rod.

When it is possible, the dry fly cast to rising fish is the most enjoyable technique. It is also the easiest of river fishing techniques, for those who can handle the tackle competently and defeat any dragging of the fly (movement of the fly at any speed other than that of the water on which it is borne) by proper line placement and subsequent manipulation.

Much off-putting nonsense has been written about dry fly fishing over the years which has created a mystique, making it seem so difficult that only the true masters can do it, and putting it far beyond the reach of the ordinary man.

In clear rivers, whether they be exclusive chalk-streams, moorland becks, or wide, rocky cascades, when a trout can be seen on the fin, lying fairly high in the water and taking the odd fly from the surface, provided the fisherman can gently present a fair likeness in size and colour of the flies the fish is taking, and without being seen – including rod, line and leader – that fish should eventually come to net. It may take patience. I have spent over an hour on a good trout in a chalk-stream and caught him on what must have been my fiftieth cast, using the same fly the whole time. The fish may miss the fly, or you may miss the trout once or twice, but that is all part of the game. Of course, it is also gratifying to take a fish with the first attempt.

Choice of fly

Just as in still waters, fish in rivers can be very choosy at times about the fly they want. This usually happens when there are a number of different flies hatching at the same time. I have found it particularly difficult in late spring on rainfed rivers, when various olives (upwing flies) and the Iron Blue are about. The trout's normal preference seems to be for the Iron Blue, and the various olives may be left alone; but the reverse can also be the case.

I confess to being a cynic, to a certain degree, about whether it is necessary to carry dozens of different fly patterns to match the various naturals exactly – or as closely as the flydressing art can come. I have always managed to hold my own – and maybe do better than most – using a very limited collection of dry flies, in shades of brown (reddish and ginger), black, buff and grey. Most of them I dress myself, not with delicate feather-fibre wings, but simply with good quality cock hackles and matching tails, slim bodies of natural and dyed herls or dubbed furs and man-made polypropylene material. I rarely dress flies to patterns in books, but simply aim at something delicate, sparkling, and which will float well.

Nor do I like the traditional winged wet flies for the subsurface style of fishing in rocky rivers. I prefer the spider-type flies with soft hackles, which *breathe* in the water and add life to the fly.

For fishing a nymph or shrimp pattern to fish lying fairly deep, but visible, I do feel that it is more important to have a pattern that closely copies the naturals. Even so, the Pheasant Tail Nymph, a similar one dressed with grey heron herls instead of cock pheasant centre tail-fibres of rusty hue, and a third of medium olive-green herl will nearly always do the trick. It is far too easy to become a fly-fiddler, wasting time tying on a dozen or so different patterns, when careful fishing with a limited range of nymphs will catch just as many fish.

However, since the idea of fishing is to have pleasure, if you get more pleasure from using a multitude of patterns, then use them. But do not become one of those pseudo-entomologists who thinks he knows just what the trout want, because none of it can ever be proved.

Tackle and presentation

Trout tackle has been described in great detail in chapter 3. Here, I would just like to discuss the best choice of tackle for river fishing. Use delicate rods, floating double-taper lines as light as will do the job, and leaders of 2.4–3.6 m (8–12 ft) long tapered to sizes suitable for use with flies that can range from size 18 up to size 10. A tippet of just over 450 g (1 lb) test may sometimes catch a fish when no heavier one will – nor any fancy fly, either.

Always approach a rising trout or a likely lie very quietly and from downstream, keeping low to prevent silhouette or shadow scaring your quarry; crawl if necessary, and wade quietly if it is permitted. Learn to cast in many ways, so that you are able to get the line flowing out through narrow gaps between trees or almost parallel to the water's surface in those well-bushed corridors of water so often found on both wild rivers and cultivated chalk rivers. Learn to cast well against the wind, which so often blows strongly downstream, and aim to let the trout see only your fly and fine tippet, never the flyline or any disturbance it may make on the water.

Opposite: Brown trout fishing on the River Kennet. If there is no bankside vegetation, you can keep a low profile by kneeling, when fishing clear, shallow streams, which reduces the height of angler and rod by half.

Delicate presentation of line, leader and fly, or flies, is as important in wet

fly and nymph fishing as it is when using the floating fly. In very strong, big rivers it is sometimes best, in order to fish the flies subsurface without any drag furrowing the surface in an unnatural way, to fish with a sinking line. But do not just cast it down and across and let it swing away below you. Fish that take the fly downstream of the rod – on the dangle, as fishermen call it – are often hooked and lost because the angle of the line pulls the fly out of the fish's mouth. It is better, even when using wet flies, to cast slightly upstream and let the flies fish down naturally to only 3.6 m (8 ft) or so below, then lift them off and cast again, preferably moving 90 cm (1 yd) or so downstream each time.

On a tiny river, a rod only 1.8 m (6 ft) long may prove a great advantage in keeping the flyline low and away from the foliage. On a big river, when wet-fly fishing upstream, a long rod – maybe 3 m (10 ft), and lissom – will help pick up the line quickly, so setting the hook into a fast-taking fish. Upstream fishing with the long rod is usually best done with a fairly short length of line out – 4.5 m (15 ft) is often enough. And it should be a light line, too, since its lack of resistance works in just the same way on the river as it does in still water. Hence the lissom rod to cast such a short, light length of line.

Although dry fly fishing is considered to be more fascinating by most fishermen, fishing a sunken nymph to a trout lying 1.2 m (4 ft) or more down, and visible as it swings from side to side to take nymphs and shrimps, is also very absorbing.

In water 1.2 m (4 ft) deep or more, a leaded nymph is often called for in any reasonable flow, but an unleaded nymph may be better in shallower water, or in water that is moving very slowly. The fly has to be cast upstream of the trout, but sink to its level as it approaches the fish. Takes can come to the drifting nymph, but it may be necessary to induce the trout to take by lifting the nymph in the water just as it gets to within 30 cm (1 ft) or so of the fish. This tactic is very deadly, but not easily done. Both the rod and the hand holding the line must work together to achieve the right motion.

Just as still-water trout in high, acid mountain lakes tend to accept surface flies when they are available, so do the wild brownies of mountain and moorland rivers that are similarly acid and lacking in the rich insect life of chalkstreams and other more alkaline waters. On Exmoor in mid-March the little browns will take dry fly in a snow-storm. One could never get the fish in a chalk-stream to rise with such freedom until May, or when the rich fly-life is beginning to hatch. In chalk-streams, there are rich pickings for the trout on the bottom and in the lush weedbeds.

For dry fly fishing on rivers, the colour of the line does not matter very much: green, brown, white or any other colour will do. The point is, never to let the trout for which you are fishing see the line, no matter what the colour.

The bright orange line – or any other colour that can be seen easily – plays its part in fishing a deep nymph. Most takes will be seen when the fish opens its mouth for the nymph, or swings aside to take it, but sometimes the fish may not be seen very easily, and then the floating part of the leader must be the tell-tale.

In clear rivers, especially chalk-streams, the depth at which the fish feeding

Opposite: Casting into the wind for brown trout, on the River Test.

on nymphs is lying, is easily underestimated, because of the clarity of the water during summer, when most nymph fishing is done. Newcomers to such rivers often try to wade in thigh-boots and find themselves waist-deep in water!

Sinking the hook

There are considerable differences between tightening to a trout taking a sunken nymph and doing so to a rise to the dry fly; and again, a difference between the right technique with dry fly on chalk-streams and on fast-flowing rain-fed rivers.

When a chalk-stream trout comes up to accept your dry fly, he is most likely to do so in a leisurely fashion, and once he has it in his mouth – and provided he feels no reason to eject it – he will slowly turn down again and move back to his lie. It is very easy to lift the rod too soon when the fish rises, with the result that the hook is either pulled out of the fish's mouth, or just takes a very light hold in the skin, or bounces off the bony framework of the jaw. It takes great control to wait that couple of seconds while the fish turns down with the fly, before sinking the barb, but that is what must be done if fish are to be hooked regularly.

On a rain-fed river, especially a small one tumbling down from high ground, trout rise much more quickly to the fast-moving fly, and perhaps because there is more competition for the available food. They are also very adept at ejecting the fly if they feel something is not quite right – and they often do. Therefore, tightening to the take of such trout must be faster, for in addition to the problem of ejection by the fish, the faster current also makes the fish move more quickly to intercept the fly. Many rises on rushing streams are sudden bursts of water; on a slower-flowing, food-rich river, rises tend to be rings, the fly being gently sipped under.

Similarly, in a chalk-stream, when a trout is seen to take the sunken nymph (by being able to watch the actions of the fish or by a signal on the leader), there is a need to tighten quickly – far more quickly than with the floating fly. This is because there is a delay period between the rod tip movement and the subsequent movement of the flyline and the leader angling down into the water. All has to be in a straight – or nearly straight – line before the movement is transmitted to the hook.

To sum up, in slow-moving rivers delay the tightening action with the dry fly but be as fast as you can with the sunken nymph. On fast rivers strike the rise to the floating fly quickly and be just as quick with takes to the wet fly and sunken nymph.

The evening rise

A well-covered stretch of the Itchen, providing shade and shelter, and an adequate flow provides food and activity.

Provided that the overhead conditions are not too bright, trout in rivers may be expected to rise to floating flies throughout most of the day, unlike the fish in many still waters, but river trout also indulge in the evening rise, especially in the period from mid-July to the end of September when sedge-flies and moths provide extra-large mouthfuls for big fish. The very big river fish usually rise only when there are plenty of these large flies about – and that is usually for a short period around dusk, although big browns may feed on well into the darkness. Provided the rules of the water permit, it is wise to fish on late in the evening.

I remember a big brown a few years ago that took a few flies during the afternoon but refused my artificials on two attempts to cover him in a little bay on the opposite bank; a cast of 18.3 m (20 yd) at that point. The intervening current was a big problem, producing drag after the fly had floated some 45 cm (18 in).

But I stayed on and caught some good fish when they began to rise to various sedges, and I heard my old friend under the other bank making great lunging rises in the gloaming. I finally tried one more cast to him and he had it right away, but he was too big and strong for me to handle in the dark and among the thick beds of ranunculus and Canadian pondweed that covered the river at that point. He ran 36.5 m (40 yd) upstream and became inextricably lodged in the weeds; a tragedy for me, since I had estimated his weight at about 2.7 kg (6 lb).

He had not minded – in fact, had obviously liked – the dragging dry sedge I had on, since the poor light had hidden any leader and other unnatural objects from his view. What I should have done, before making that attempt, was to exchange the 1.3 kg (3 lb) leader, on which I had landed fish to 1.8 kg (4 lb) that day, for something more in keeping with his stature!

Some river flyfishers still adhere to the misconception that their trout are wild and more difficult to catch than those in reservoirs, but the sad truth today is that most of the expensive and beautiful chalk-streams are stocked with the very same trout that are put into the reservoirs, because fishing pressure is too great for natural spawning to keep pace with. Both browns and rainbows are put into the best chalk-streams today, although many fishermen are against rainbow stocking. A few rivers – such as the upper Avon in Wiltshire and the Itchen – contain mostly brown trout, but comparatively few of them are wild-bred fish.

Chapter Six

Going fishing: typical experiences on rivers

Most chalk-stream and limestone river fishing does not begin until 1 May – or even a little later – although some rivers open in April. Chalk-stream fishermen, however, prefer to use the dry fly, and since regular rises seldom begin until May, most of them do not start to fish until that lovely month.

By that time, hatches of fly should be quite good, with Medium Olives, Pale Watery Olives and Iron Blues showing well. Black Gnats, a land-bred fly that trout love to take, are also likely to be about.

Unless the Pale Wateries are hatching in profusion, a dark fly is usually the best dry fly choice; something about size 14. Greenwell's Glory, Gold-ribbed Hare's Ear and Iron Blue are good patterns to have, although quite often any small fly of similar colouring will catch fish. I like the dry Pheasant Tail and the trout seem to approve, too.

Chalk-streams

To give an example of how, sometimes, trout on chalk-streams behave with what could be construed as stupidity, I remember on one occasion catching a few fish using a size 14 dry fly that was simply a slim body of natural grey heron herl with a pale, gingery hackle, a few fibres of which also formed the tail. After lunch, however, fish began to refuse this fly, and several others that I tried. Just for fun, I put on a size 14 dry fly which had a body of dubbed wild rabbit fur, including some of the blue-grey underfur and some of the black-fawn guard hairs, with a tiny hackle of hot-orange dyed cock. Fish took that as if they had been waiting for it all their lives, but I know of no natural fly that looks like that.

Wild browns on wild rivers can also be rather unpredictable. Once, on the upper Teifi near Tregaron, the wild browns began rising to olives of various pale and dark shades, and I found a Ginger Quill good medicine. They then became increasingly choosy and, in desperation, I tied on a size 12 Grey Wulff, a fuzzy American pattern devised by Lee Wulff with brown squirrel-tail hair for wings – a real 'haystack' of a fly but one that floats really well in rough water. It caught me several good fish.

Dave Collyer, the excellent British flydresser, once used another of the Wulff series, a White Wulff, to take a couple of 450 g (1 lb) plus wild browns

Above: A delightful little pool on a moorland stream produced a lively 225 g (½ lb) fish in March for the author, seen using a light bamboo rod.

Left: Trout fishing by Ovington Mill, on the Itchen.

from Exmoor's tiny River Barle, and this was a size 10 fly where a 14 is normally required. The Barle trout are tiny, so a 25 cm (10 in) fish is a whopper!

It pays not to be too hidebound about dry fly patterns, even though it is very rewarding to establish what fly the fish are taking, tie on an artificial that looks similar, and find that it works.

A pattern which I would not like to be without on any river is Lunn's Caperer, which is supposed to represent a sedge. It has one hackle of black cock and a second of medium Rhode Island Red cock, the body being of brown turkey-tail fibres with a median band of yellow swan herl. It is a bulky fly but it works even when no sedges or look-alike flies are on the water.

Lunn's Caperer has taken fish for me on chalk-streams and wild hill streams, but the success I remember best was on a river in south-east England that, in its upper reaches, contains one trout to every 500 or so chub, dace, roach and other coarse fish. That afternoon, on the upper Medway, I caught two trout, of 680 g and 570 g (1½ and 1¼ lb) – very good for the river – on a Caperer when nothing else brought any response. I also lost two other trout, including a fish of close to 900 g (2 lb). Chub and dace also took the Caperer on that hot, bright afternoon, and I have reached the conclusion that something about this fly makes it, at times, irresistible to fish.

Well oiled, the Caperer and any other fuzzy, sedge-imitating pattern can be deadly for trout in smooth, gliding water at dusk, when they are cast almost straight across the current with the line being allowed to belly downstream. The fly is dragged over the surface, making a wake which simulates the wake of a natural sedge-fly trying to take off. Hand-stripping may also be in order, although some chalk-stream purists would frown upon such tactics.

In high summer, when the streams are low and very clear, daytime fishing with the sunk nymph can be quite fascinating. If you are able to 'Indian' to within 4.5 m (5 yd) or so downstream of a good trout hanging near the bottom in 90 cm (3 ft) or more of water, darting from side to side to take nymphs and shrimps swept down by the current or nosing the weeds for them, and can cast a nymph so that it comes down to the fish at his depth, maybe just drifting, maybe lifting before his eyes, it can be very exciting. Every fin-beat, every gill-movement, is visible.

However, while the fish are visible to the fisherman, so are the careless movements of the fisherman to the fish. Once, when fishing the Kennet in such conditions towards the end of September, I found several fish nymphing but nearly every time I cast, I scared them. I knew they had not seen my line or leader and I wondered what I was doing wrong. I sat down on the bank and tried to solve the problem.

I had taken two nice fish early in the morning when the air was a little chill, and since it had become warmer I had put my green pullover in my waistcoat back-pocket. I wondered: was it because I was now fishing in shirt-sleeve order? Were my bare arms frightening the fish as I cast to them from short range? It was necessary to get close to the fish in order to see both where to cast, and when they took the nymph.

I put my pullover back on, and took the next two trout without any problems. Since then, I have always worn a long-sleeved green or khaki shirt for fishing at close quarters in warm weather, and I am convinced that the change has made a great difference to my success rate.

Rain-fed rivers

One May morning, about noon, I arrived on a lovely stretch of the Scottish Tweed above Peebles to find trout ringing the river in an almost constant pattern. Hundreds of olives were coming down, like little yachts, in the spring sunshine and I tied on a matching Ginger Quill, a commercially dressed one with a small upright wing of dark blue feather, and commenced to cast to two dozen or so fish rising consistently in a small pool overhung with alders. After nearly an hour, during which I must have covered various fish more than fifty times, with only one splashy rise to my fly and the fish coming off almost immediately, I again waded to the bank, as is my normal procedure, to smoke and consider the problem.

I then noticed that, among the rafts of dark olives coming down, were a few Iron Blues. I switched to a size 16 fly with a thinly-dubbed body of blue wild rabbit underfur and a dark grey hackle of two jackdaw hackles.

It worked, of course, and had I not paused to ponder the problem, I probably would have flogged away fruitlessly with the fly I *thought* they were taking instead of a pattern similar to the one they *were* selecting.

Opposite: Fishing for wild brown trout on the River Exe, below Exmoor.

The Lune is a lovely spate river with good brown trout; truly wild fish that can pull twice their weight, it seems. A few years ago, it was also full of spring salmon and, later, a large number of moderate seatrout together with some very big specimens. In recent years, following the disease Ulcerative Dermal Necrosis, Lune salmon fishing has been a mere shadow of what it used to be, but the brownies have remained plentiful and in fine fettle.

When I first fished the river, I took with me many small traditional wet flies, winged and hackled, and had a few small trout – and many unproductive pulls – for my efforts. It was not until my host, Reg Righyni, showed me the tiny, sparsely-dressed spider-flies used on that river and on other northern spate streams, that I tried them myself. What a revelation the trout's response was, to such wisps of feather, fur and silk.

Snipe and Purple, Poult Bloa, Partridge and Orange were the ones that served me best, fished on point and dropper with 1.3 kg (3 lb) nylon, or a little less. Nothing above size 14 would interest the fish, and size 16 was better. Cast gently across the fast streams and being allowed to drift down, just subsurface, with a light, floating line, they brought quicksilver rises and pulls that required speed to hook. In spots where I had previously drawn blanks with my heavily-dressed south country flies, I would now catch maybe a dozen browns, fish of 170 g to close on 450 g (6 oz–1 lb) as a rule, though I took fish over 450 g (1 lb), too.

On a couple of occasions, while idling away an hour in the late evening before beginning the more serious seatrout fishing, I took seatrout on these tiny flies and light leaders that careered all over the river before being led to the net. Reg had caught at least one of 1.8 kg (4 lb) grilse on such a fly and light nylon, in perhaps 60 cm (2 ft) of fast-flowing water – fishing for trout, of course.

I have spent some time discussing suitable tackle earlier on, but there is one point to be made here about fishing small spate streams, and even the feeders and carriers of the chalk-streams. Quite often, the length of flyline one can get outside the rod tip when casting on these tiny streams is only 1.8 m (2 yd) or so, and that weight of line, if it is matched to the rod in the normal way, is insufficient to flex the rod. One answer is to use a cane rod of 1.8–2.1 m (6–7 ft) with a very easy action; I have found the Hardy 'Marvel' excellent. Such a rod performs a casting action, without the weight of a line on it, due to its own weight – something a hollow-glass or graphite rod will seldom do. The alternative is to use a rod for a number 3 with a number 4 or even a 5 line.

For this type of fishing, and for some chalk-stream dry fly work where one casts very few times in a day (and then only to fish seen to rise), the good split-cane rod has a place. Its weight is not excessive in the lengths and for the line sizes used, and the help that the slow, smooth action gives, especially on little streams overgrown with trees, more than compensates for any extra weight on the wrist.

PART TWO

Seatrout and salmon

Chapter Seven

Seatrout

According to zoologists, the seatrout is simply a brown trout that migrates to the sea to take advantage of the rich feeding. Both the brown trout and the seatrout have the same scientific name: *Salmo trutta*.

It is said that seatrout evolved due to the lack of an adequate food supply in some of the acid mountain rivers, so that starving brown trout dropped downstream, eventually to go to sea to feed, returning to the rivers to spawn in late autumn and going back to the sea again in spring. Unlike the salmon, the seatrout often spawns every year and mortality from spawning is rare.

While the seatrout is similar to the brown trout in body shape, it is more like the salmon in colouration when it first runs into the river, usually from late May to late September, being silver and lilac with a dark blue back and black spots, like asterisks, both above and below the lateral line. Having been in freshwater for a month or so, the seatrout loses its silvery sheen and becomes darker, more like a non-migratory brown trout. In fact, it can even develop dark-red spots like the freshwater brown trout.

However, from a fisherman's point of view, the seatrout's behaviour is as unlike that of a brown trout as that of a fox and the family's pet poodle. Both fish can be wary, but the seatrout is far more retiring and easily scared than a brown trout and its strength and stamina on the hook is almost beyond compare. Its speed is astonishing, its leaps acrobatic. And when it is fresh-run its flesh is as pink-orange as that of any salmon, and many gourmets prefer its flavour above all other.

Undoubtedly some seatrout feed in freshwater, but the less so the longer they have spent in the river. None of the seatrout taken from certain rivers that I have fished have ever, on post-mortem examination, been found to contain any food. I have also caught seatrout on maggots and worms, and have seen many others taken, which had been feeding heavily on maggots used as groundbait by coarse fishermen.

Seatrout usually spawn in clean rivers in November and December, although some spawn as late as February. Seatrout progeny are also migratory and, after an average of three years spent feeding just like brown trout in the river, they become silvery and, at 15–20 cm (6–8 in) in length, make their first journey, as smolts, to the sea. This generally happens in late spring and some of the little fish may return to the river within a few months, having grown to 2.5 cm (10 in) or so. Others remain in the sea for one to four years before returning as lusty fish weighing 2–3 kg (4–6 lb). The seatrout's ways are unpredictable.

And that is really sufficient background on the seatrout. It is now necessary to discuss its behaviour relative to the sport of flyfishing.

A seatrout river may be a wild Scottish, Irish or Welsh mountain river or a Hampshire chalk-stream with access to the sea. Seatrout are happy to run a river and then spend some time in natural lakes in the river's course before running up feeders and headwaters to spawn. Seatrout will run up torrents but they prefer, once there, to remain in the more gently-flowing water, preferably with overhead cover in the form of trees.

They have been successfully transplanted to other parts of the world and the huge fish of the Falkland Islands and in the Tierra del Fuego rivers of South America are legendary.

Most seatrout flyfishing is done with so-called wet flies, although some of them are more like the reservoir fisherman's lures, including tandem hooks; but the dry fly also works, usually in daylight, and in Norway it is a favourite technique. The dry fly is also effective when boat fishing on the drift on lakes and lochs holding seatrout, although such floating flies are more often fished by dapping with a rod of 3.95 m (13 ft) or more and a thick but light floss blowline. Effective as these big dry flies are, skittered along the surface with the dapping outfit, it is not really flyfishing, which demands the line be cast rather than blown out by the wind.

Rivers

The flyfisher's seatrout season generally begins in June during warm, settled weather. Fish have begun to move into the rivers and to settle down in the pools. In many rivers seatrout fishing is an after-dark pursuit and few people bother to fish in the daytime.

The night may seem dark to the human eye but to the seatrout it is obviously not. For not only does the seatrout see flies crossing his vision near to the surface while he lies near the riverbed, perhaps 1.2 m (4 ft) or more below, but he can also see a dark, silver-bodied fly at eye level in 1.8 m (6 ft) of water on the blackest night nature ever made.

The seatrout's night vision – if that is what guides him to the fly – is not his only asset. He can detect the rattle of a heavy footfall on the bank or wading on the gravels; he can be scared by ripples caused by careless wading, or the movement of a human form or rod against the sky. A flyline splashing down on the water can ruin prospects for an hour or more. In seatrout flyfishing, stealth and concealment are of prime importance.

It is folly to fish the fly for seatrout at night in high and coloured water. The river must be clear and fairly low. The fish may take a fly in the daylight when the river carries extra water and a tinge of colour, but not at night. Yet on many rain-fed rivers running over moorland, good conditions occur when the spate is beginning to fall and the water is clearing from a dark winey colour to that of pale sherry. A good indication of the right night-fishing conditions is when moths begin to flutter as dusk approaches, when bats come out before

the light has gone, and when you do not feel the need to don an extra sweater or a coat before beginning to fish.

The usual pattern of a good seatrout night, like that described above, begins with the noisy sploshing of seatrout at dusk. Wait until it is really dark before starting to fish; beginning too early can ruin the pool by scaring fish. It is best to inspect the pool closely in daylight, so that casting distances to the far bank and under the trees where most good lies are found, can be planned. Watch out for riverbed snags and deep holes that can be a danger after dark. Mark any problem areas with a stick stuck in the bank that can be found later as a guide. Try a few casts to get the range right, if you feel so inclined; a short length of cotton whipped round the line at the point between reel and butt ring when the longest cast is made can be felt after dark and prevent overcasting into the trees.

When darkness falls, rivers that all day saw only the salmon leaping and maybe small trout dimpling the surface, suddenly come alive. Seatrout splash and slosh in the tails of the pools, often with a strange whirring sound that is made by the fishs' vibrating tails as they clear the water.

The conditions that bring about this nocturnal seatrout activity are periods of warm and settled weather with cloud cover that prevents sudden drops in temperature after sunset. Seatrout are highly susceptible to sudden temperature changes and even a reduction of a couple of degrees in air temperature can cause all the surface activity to stop. However, some of the fish may still take a deeply-fished fly. Low water conditions are better than high, but low water does not mean streams reduced to a trickle. Low summer flow is what is required.

Big seatrout – fish of 5 kg (11 lb) or more – will run up insignificant little rivers. A stream that is generally less than 90 cm (3 ft) deep and rarely wider than 7.6 m (25 ft) can hold huge fish. But so can rivers that are wide and fast and deep – like the Scottish Spey, for example.

Obviously, with these widely differing river conditions, the flyfishers' tackle must also vary. On a little stream a rod of 2.45 m (8 ft) and a size 5 line might be ideal, whereas on a wide river, where wading is required to cover the water adequately, a rod of 3.05 m (10 ft) and a size 7 line might be needed. The latter outfit would be fine, too, for lough fishing from a boat.

The size of fly being used also affects the rod and line used. A rod of 2.45 m (8 ft) with a size 5 line will be right for a little river when using size 10 traditional wet flies, such as Teal, Blue and Silver, Butcher, Peter Ross and Mallard and Claret, for example. Casting distances may be quite short – maybe never more than 6 m (20 ft). On the other hand, trying to fish a tandem-hooked lure 6.5 cm (2½ in) long near the gravel in a wide pool, where the casting distance is 18.3 m (20 yd) or more, demands a longer, stiffer rod, a size 7 sinking line and a leader that will not fold up under the weight of the big, air-resistant fly. It is the same story as that of reservoir trout fishing.

Most seatrout flies, wet flies that is, need to be long and slim with plenty of silver tinsel on the bodies and with a dark outline easily seen in silhouette by the fish against the light source.

It is best to carry all you need in pockets; again, a bag on the bank is the

In fast water it is best, when fishing alone, to steer the fish upstream of the waiting net, then let the current wash it back into the extended mesh.

cause of excessive water disturbance if you need to wade in and out to get more flies, spare nylon, and so on. Carry a small pen-type torch, but never shine it over the water. And use it as little as possible: night vision can become very good after a while, but a light will ruin it for quite a long time. The torch should be used only for tying on a new fly, for untangling a leader or for unhooking and dispatching a fish.

In addition to rod, reel, lines on spare spools, leaders, flies, landing net and other accessories that will obviously be needed, always carry some good anti-midge cream or spray since the riverside on a warm night can be hell with biting insects. And take plenty of food and hot drink; a long night's fishing is very tiring and food and drink can keep the body and the mind active. Brief rest periods, both to sustain oneself and rest the pool, are never wasted.

At night, seatrout tend to move out from under their daytime cover, trees, high banks, rocks and deep holes, and fall back to the smooth-flowing shallow water and the tails of pools. Good fish will be taken in water only 60 cm (2 ft) deep and I recommend that you start with a double-taper floating line and one wet fly. Seatrout sometimes accept tiny brown trout flies – size 14 – in daylight, but at night something with more bulk usually does best, and a size 6 or 8 is a good one to start with. A size 4 may do better. Try all three sizes, and drop down to a 10, if you feel the need.

The leader need be no longer than 3 m (10 ft) when using a rod of that length; for a 2.45 m (8 ft) rod, a leader of 2.7 m (9 ft) will be found reasonable. Only use the short rod on streams that average 7.6 m (25 ft) in width; a good happy-medium rod for seatrout is 2.90 m (9½ ft) with a size 6 or 7 line. Because it may be necessary to battle in the dark with a fish of 4.5 kg (10 lb) or more – and many small rivers hold fish of that weight – a tippet of 2.2–2.7 kg (5–6 lb) should be used. On rivers where big fish are common – such as Wales' Conway, Towey, Dovey and Dwyfawr – or when using sunk line and/or a lure 5 cm (2 in) or more long, I would always plump for a 3.1 kg (7 lb) tippet.

The scheme should entail casting downstream and across, setting the line down as gently as possible, and then letting the flow fish the fly across the river. In slow water it may be necessary to increase the fishing speed of the fly by stripping smoothly with the free hand. Try to make the fly move at the same smooth speed across the river, which may mean stripping it when you feel the tension of the current's pull on the line slackening as the line and fly fish round into your bank.

The floating line will fish the fly between 5 cm (2 in) and 30 cm (1 ft) below the surface, depending on the size (weight) of the fly and current speed. As I have already said, a slim-profile fly is called for, since a bulky fly will tend to be forced to the surface where it will cause a wake. A wake is sometimes attractive to night seatrout, but that is another technique, which will be dealt with later. With the normal wet fly, a subsurface presentation is what is needed.

Start at the chosen place at the upstream end of the stretch of water and make at least three casts to the same place from one position before taking a couple of slow, gentle paces downstream. You may be wading thigh-deep or you may be on the bank. No matter what, move with stealth.

Opposite: Seatrout fishing from a boat on the Hampshire Avon.

Takes vary considerably, from a great pull that almost has the rod from your hand to a gentle stopping of the line in its swing across the current. It may, in the latter case, be a snag that has caught the fly, or a floating piece of debris, but tighten anyway. Sometimes, when the fly is fishing very close to the surface, the fish will splash as it takes the fly. Always fish the fly right round to your own bank, or downstream of your wading position, and then, when it is on the dangle, draw line in slow, smooth strips for a metre or so before lifting off for the next cast. A fish may follow the fly in and will turn away if its progress slows down in the shallow, slack water. Keep the fly moving temptingly.

Periodically check the hook point, specially if the fly is often felt touching rocks or the gravel bed. And check, too, when you feel the fly touch something – bank or branches – on a back-cast. A sharp hook point is essential, as always. It is surprising how a mere tap felt on the back-cast can mean that the whole point of the hook has broken off. Seatrout will still take the broken fly, but you will never hook the fish.

On a good night, the floating line will often catch fish until well after midnight, after which there may be a period when the splashes and takes tail off to nothing. That is a good time to take a rest. The fish may begin splashing again after half an hour, or less, or it might be an hour. Begin fishing again, whether the fish are active or not, with the floating line, but if nothing happens, change tactics.

It is likely that the temperature has fallen and the fish have stopped moving actively, lying closer to the riverbed. The sunk line is now the best move. The lure, between 5–6.5 cm ($2-2\frac{1}{2}$ in) long, should be dressed on two downward-facing hooks, size 8 for the 5 cm (2 in) fly, 6 for the longer one, linked by 11.3 kg (25 lb) monofilament nylon on to which the hookshanks are securely whipped using a spot of Super Glue 3 or Araldite. The dressing is simple: both hook shanks are covered with silver tinsel and the throat hackle is turquoise-blue cock with a wing of dark mallard feather or of dark brown squirrel tail hair, or bucktail.

This fishy-looking creation, swinging across the river near the bottom and confronting the fish at eyeball level, is thought to produce a strong predatory reaction from the fish, which seizes it, it seems, usually as it has just passed the lie and appears to be getting away.

Many of us have to take our seatrout fishing as it comes and, having travelled maybe 300 miles to the river, we want to fish, even if conditions are not right. For example, arriving to find the evening temperature falling and with little or no signs of surface activity by the seatrout, I would set up for sunk-line fishing immediately, rather than begin with the floating line. As has often been said, there are as many fools in the water as there are on the bank and even in cold conditions, or with the river running a little too high, or with no overhead cloud and maybe an excess of moonlight – which is usually bad for results – I would hope for at least some reaction from the fish when fishing a lure just above the riverbed.

In these unfavourable conditions, it pays to fish a little higher up the pool than one would in good conditions, where the water is a little deeper. The best prospects when there is too much moonlight occur where the fly can be fished under trees or high banks that overshadow the water.

Where daytime flyfishing for seatrout is practised, the usual technique is very much like wet fly fishing down and across for brown trout. Smaller flies than are used for night fishing will usually be found more acceptable by the fish and I have had good sport with small fish – 450–900 kg (1–2 lb) – using size 14 North Country spider-type trout flies on a floating line.

Before leaving the subject of river fishing, I should mention the night-fishing tactic of the wake fly. On a very dark night and when the fish are fickle, a big fly fished across the smooth flow, so that it creates a wake, can be extremely deadly – and occasionally a salmon will take it in addition to seatrout. Maybe the fish think the wake is made by a big night-flying sedge fly scuttering across the surface, or maybe something even more substantial, like a big beetle.

The fly must be big and bulky. Special wake flies have heads of cork, or balsa wood, or plastic foam and are dressed on long-shanked hooks, about size 4, usually with another similar size hook in tandem behind it – as for the sunk lure – or with a size 10 or 12 treble hook behind the single hook. Overall length is about 6.4 cm (2½ in). Some of the American popping bugs, used for black bass fishing, may be used, or a well-greased Muddler Minnow, or even a greased fuzzy dry fly, such as an overdressed Palmer pattern, will often do the trick. The main point is that the fly must remain afloat and making a wake.

Obviously the floating line is called for and, like the sunk fly and lure, the pace of the wake fly must be fairly constant. In places where the water slows considerably near one's own bank, the fly must be stripped to continue the wake. Sometimes the fish want the fly coming across simply dragged by the belly of the line in the flow, without any manipulation of the line; at others a smooth, fast stripping action may prove just what the fish want. Always experiment; the unconventional tactic is often the one that catches fish in difficult conditions.

Still waters

Seatrout fishing in loughs and lochs is usually done from a drifting boat over rocky or gravelly shallow areas and in the region of outflowing and inflowing rivers and feeders. The best areas of each water are known to local anglers and professional gillies and a chat with the first over a drink is never a wasted investment. There are both good and bad gillies, and a good one is well worth his hire, if you can afford it.

Good lake (loch/lough) conditions are a south-westerly breeze making a nice ripple on the water, with changing clouds covering intermittent sunshine and maybe the odd warm shower. The boat is drifted beam-on down the wind over recognized seatrout lies and it may be controlled by the gillie with the oars or with a drogue, depending on the wind strength and the intended path of the boat over the holding ground.

Rods of 3.05–3.35 m (10–11 ft) are customary and usually with a DT6/7 line, which may be a floater, a sink-tip or a sinker. Two flies are usually fished and the dropper is brought back to dibble the surface near the boat, just as in lake fishing for brown trout. Sometimes seatrout will be seen to rise, just like

A good breeze is breaking up the surface of Lake Voshimid as these fishermen cast for seatrout.

brown trout, and such movements should be covered quickly and the flies fished quite fast over the spot.

Provided there is a ripple, the wind that makes it can be relatively unimportant: some lakes fish well in a northerly or north-westerly breeze. Easterly winds are not conducive to good fishing as a rule – but rules are often thrown aside.

A flat calm in bright sunshine is regarded as almost hopeless for lake seatrout fishing from a boat – and few bother to fish from the shores of these vast Scottish and Irish lakes. But I can remember one such day when I cast a size 12 Invicta from a rocky shoreline where I could see down some 3 m (10 ft), so clear was the water and the light penetration was so good. I fished with a floating line and a 4.2 m (14 ft) leader with a 1.8 kg (4 lb) tippet and hooked two good fish within half an hour. Unfortunately both decided that they wanted to be some 90 m (100 yd) from where they made their mistakes, and the light tippet parted when a long length of flyline and backing created too much resistance for the nylon to withstand. However, I did hook those fish and both were good for the particular lake – one was about 1.8 kg (4 lb), the other nearer to 2.7 kg (6 lb). I saw the first one come up to take the little fly from some 2.4 m (8 ft) down.

In a really big wave, a Palmer-dressed dry fly, such as a Zulu or similar, well greased and skimmed across the waves, will often take fish where the usual subsurface fly will not.

Wherever you flyfish for seatrout, never underestimate the fight-power of these fish. Few fish can run so far and so fast, nor can they leap so high and shake out hooks so well. I am never happy with less than 90 m (100 yd) of 6.8–9 kg (15–20 lb) test braided Terylene backing behind my flyline when seatrout fishing. And even if the seatrout on the water being fished are small on average – say 900 g–1.8 kg (2–4 lb) – there is always the chance of hooking a bigger fish, or a salmon.

Estuaries

Both in the river and on lakes, the seatrout that take most frequently are those which have been in freshwater the shortest time. It therefore seems obvious that if we fish for them in the sea – or in an estuary – our chances are better than in freshwater. And in many places, such is the case.

While in saltwater, seatrout feed heavily on sand-eels, small fish such as sprats and herring fry, shrimps and prawns. The best flies for use in saltwater or brackish estuarine water, therefore, are those that look like sand-eels, small fish or shrimps and prawns – lures, in fact, from 6.5–9 cm (2½–3½ in) in length.

Both rocky, weedy estuaries and shallow, sandy ones can produce seatrout and since long casting may be called for, and because we need to make our lures appear like small fish or crustaceans darting through the water among the rocks, weeds and over the sand, we can strip them, just like in still-water trout fishing with the lure. And that indicates the need to use a weight-forward or shooting-taper line, a floater, maybe, or a sink-tip or full sinker, depending on the depth of the water and its flow.

Fishing some estuaries with strongly flowing water can be accomplished by standing on the shore or by wading and casting a long line across the current and stripping the fly back fairly slowly, the current also fishing the fly attractively down and across, as in the river. However, in some estuaries there may be areas of almost lake-like water where seatrout are feeding and here the true still-water lure method is called for.

Calm, warm weather is once again best for saltwater fishing and some sunshine, provided there is a ripple on the water, seems beneficial. The periods around dawn and again at dusk are excellent and the very best fishing can occur when the river itself is almost at drought level so that seatrout stocks build up in the estuary. When the river is high, estuary fishing is usually a waste of time, since the fish will be more interested in running upstream than feeding in the saltwater.

The period from halfway down the ebb tide until an hour after dead low water is generally best for estuary and saltwater fishing. The ebb tide exposes large areas of seatrout water and makes it accessible to the fisherman as he wades carefully, casting to likely spots. Likely spots may be rocky projections into the tideway or giving access to other low-lying weed-draped rocks, or large, shallow pools left by the tide, or the places where small freshwater streams run into the sea.

Some sandy estuaries have a sandbar near their mouths and at low water it is sometimes possible to wade along the bar and cast into the rough water on the seaward side. Always beware, when fishing estuaries, of the tide: it is very easy to become cut off by the rising water. For this reason it is safer to make it a rule to fish with a companion.

A bonus in estuaries often comes in the form of a bass or mackerel, both of which provide excellent fishing on the tackle used. In deep, rocky estuaries pollack, too, will sometimes be taken.

Night fishing also produces good sport in saltwater, but again be very careful not to wade too deeply or get cut off by a flooding tide. Another hazard is that of getting a foot trapped between rocks. Try to fish from the shore or marginal shallows in the darkness rather than risk an accident. However, in some shallow, sandy estuaries, wading at night can be fairly safe, provided a weather-eye is kept on the tide.

While the latter half of the ebb tide and the low water period is generally most productive, there are places where the fish only move into range towards high water. Such places include tiny bays with streams running into them or even long inlets on salt marshes.

While fly dressings are given in a separate chapter, I must mention here that I would be happy to fish just two patterns for all estuary and saltwater seatrouting. The first is a 3.5–7.5 cm ($1\frac{1}{2}$–3 in) tandem-hook lure with silver tinsel bodies and a wing, tied to reach the bend of the rear hook, made from two turquoise-dyed cock hackles, tied with their curves inwards, with two badger hackles (white with a black central stripe) outside them and also back to back, with a long, slim bunch of black or brown squirrel or bucktail over the top to form a kind of 'roof'. The other is on a similar tandem-hook arrangement with silver bodies, but the cock hackles are white, two on each side, with a 'roof' of plain grey squirrel hair and a slim beard hackle of hot-orange cock hackle fibres; size 8 hooks up to 5 cm (2 in), 6 for 6.5 and 7.5 cm ($2\frac{1}{2}$ and 3 in).

A final point about catching seatrout in the sea: no seatrout you catch in the river will have such beauty, such a wonderful shape, will fight so hard. Seatrout from saltwater have a silver, lilac, dark blue and pinkish glow about them that is never found in a fish in the river, even taken low down when it has been in freshwater only a few hours.

And the fishing in estuarine water is usually free, provided there is access to the areas you wish to fish. It is also a part of seatrout fishing that remains relatively unexplored. There is, however, one important fact to remember: saltwater is highly corrosive and all tackle, rod, reel and even the flies used, must be thoroughly washed in warm freshwater and dried after use. Reels should be carefully oiled; aluminium alloys are quickly damaged by seawater. Plastic-covered modern flylines, however, take no harm from saltwater, but they should be stripped from the reel, washed and dried, and rewound, to prevent salt on the line attracting moisture and corroding the reel.

Chapter Eight
Salmon

Salmon fishing is a world apart. It is different from all other types of angling because the Atlantic salmon, *Salmo salar*, does not feed in freshwater. The fact that a salmon will take into its mouth a bunch of live worms, a long-dead prawn or shrimp, a wooden, plastic or metal spinner, or other lure, or an angler's artificial fly, is something not far short of a miracle. It is also a miracle that a salmon may swim up a river in January and spawn in November when the year is dying, and do so without having eaten anything at all in the eleven months between.

So why does the salmon take a bait or an artificial lure? Some say it is due to the fish's memory of its rich sea feeding on herrings, other fish, molluscs and crustaceans, and that its acceptance is an involuntary one. Others hold that the memory that moves the salmon to take bait or lure is one of its youth, after its birth in the river, following which, rather like the young seatrout, it feeds like a brown trout on shrimps, nymphs and all manner of riverlife, to grow into a smolt and migrate to the sea, some to journey across the Atlantic and feed on the almost untapped larders beneath the polar ice.

No matter what makes the fish accept bait or lure, the fact that he does so allows us to catch him. And the sooner we can present our hook to him after he has entered the river, the more likely we are to catch him.

Atlantic salmon inhabit the rivers of north-west Europe and some on the eastern seaboard of the North American continent. Wherever they are found, they spawn in the rivers in autumn and winter, migrate to the Atlantic, then return, usually (but not always) to the rivers of their origin, to spawn. Many die from the rigours of spawning, but five per cent survive to spawn a second time. The various salmon species of the Pacific never survive spawning. They all die.

Because the prime pink flesh of the salmon is considered such a delicacy, man has overexploited the species. For many years it has been caught in nets and traps on its return to the rivers, and in more recent years it has been taken in vast numbers on the high seas, particularly at its feeding grounds in the Davis Strait off Greenland, or on its migration paths to the area. Modern science, with its various tracking devices and sophisticated fishing methods, has reduced the world's stocks of this wonderful fish to a level that is low enough to worry even the scientists who permitted the damage.

Since the fish probably home on their natal rivers by smelling the special water-scent of the rivers, in countries where overfishing, pollution and similar ills, including water abstraction, have been permitted to go on uncontrolled, the salmon have, to all intents and purposes, ceased to exist. Spain, France and Ireland have badly damaged their own resources. Spain and France have little to offer the fisherman now; Ireland's fishing is a mere shadow of its once-magnificent past.

Only in Iceland is the salmon picture a bright one. There, because of strict controls of the resource, which brings the fish-dependent island much revenue from sport-fishermen, salmon have been steadily increasing. So has the quality of the angling. In North American rivers there has been some improvement; there, angling for salmon is permitted only with the fly. The numbers of fish anglers are allowed to take are also strictly controlled.

Life cycle

Like the other salmonids, the Atlantic salmon spawn in clean rivers with rocky, gravelly beds. The hen fish digs a trough in the gravels by tail movements that dislodge stones with the aid of water pressure, and lays her eggs in the trough, which are simultaneously fertilized by the milt of the cock salmon; and by precocious male salmon parr getting in on the act. She then leaves them to their fate. Spent, and called a kelt, she tries to regain the sea and feed herself up again for another journey of procreation. The cock fish remain to fertilize the eggs of other females before they, too, try to regain the sea. Very few make it. Hens have a recovery rate at least three times as good as that of the males.

The eggs hatch in the gravels – having been covered with stones by the hen fish – into tiny fish called alevins, with a sustaining food supply in a yolk sac. When the sac's supply has been absorbed, the fish is called a parr, with dark markings, like finger-prints, along its flanks. It feeds in the river, for from one to five years, depending on the quality of the food-stock, then migrates to sea as a smolt, usually at a length of 15–20 cm (6–8 in), and begins the life-cycle all over again.

The salmon return to their natal rivers after between one and five years feeding at sea. They may weigh as little as about 1.3 kg (3 lb) or as much as nearly 22 kg (50 lb). The record fly-caught salmon came from Norway's Aäro River and weighed 34 kg (76 lb); the biggest rod-caught salmon from British waters was a 29 kg (64 lb) fish from the Scottish Tay, which was caught on spinning tackle by a woman.

Big salmon – usually fish over 4.5 kg (10 lb) – run the rivers in the cold months of the year, usually from January until May and again in October and November. Smaller salmon generally run in summer, and fish which have spent only one full year, or a little more, in the sea before making their first return journey are termed grilse. They are usually slim, bright fish and run in June and July, as a rule. There is always, however, an overlap, and a 13.6 kg (30 lb) fish may be caught in midsummer.

Big rivers usually produce big salmon; small spate rivers, such as those on Scotland's west coast, are run by mature fish that may rarely exceed 4.5 kg (10 lb). A salmon's size is dependent on how long it has spent at sea, feeding on the nourishing food there.

Opposite, above: With plenty of room between them, the two salmon fishermen work down Hafod Pool of the Gwydyr Hotel water of the Conway near Betws-y-Coed in North Wales. The man following down was wading as deeply as any man the author has ever seen, anywhere!

Opposite, below: Salmon like to lie in shadow, if they can, and suitable flow beneath trees, under bridges, high rocks and other natural and man-made features is always worth trying. Here the author fishes floating line on the Irish Blackwater near Ballyhooly.

The salmon fisherman never tires of seeing this spectacle: a running salmon leaping an obstacle on its upstream migration.

Later summer and autumn grayling fishing with the fly, both dry and sunken nymph, is excellent sport in colourful surroundings. Here B.H. fishes the Test.

Salmon-fishing seasons open at various times. Some rivers open in January and close in October, others open in March and close at the end of September, and some open in April and close in mid-December. Seasons are usually based on the local running times of fresh fish and some rivers are not considered to be worth fishing until the period July to September, these usually being the small spate rivers.

Water temperature and clarity, the latter to a lesser extent, are the key to salmon flyfishing tactics. In the cold waters of January to April, when most rivers will be carrying extra water, the fly generally needs to be big and easily seen, and to be fished very close to the bottom, where the fish will be lying, a little out of the main rush of water. Salmon in the cold water of February and March – optimistically called spring by salmon addicts – are rather lethargic and will not chase all over the river to take the fly.

The fly itself might need to be 7.5 cm (3 in) long, or even a little more, with plenty of yellow, orange or blue in its make-up, to show up better in the coloured water. Fished as slowly across the river as possible, and aimed to pass just in front of the salmon's nose, such a fly is a good taker of these usually big fish in cold water.

Left and above: Roll-casting with a trout rod is well illustrated here by Donald Downs – even though he is one of those rare southpaws.

From the middle of April onwards, as the water warms up, the salmon are more likely to move to intercept a fly, either across the stream or from deep down to take near the surface, and the fly can be progressively smaller as the water gets warmer until, in a hot June, the most killing fly might be a wisp of hair and feather only 12 mm ($\frac{1}{2}$ in) long, or slightly less.

Fresh-run salmon take much more readily than those that have been in the river a long time. They also take best when they first enter the pool being fished.

Tackle and accessories

Once again, the size of the fly being used, the depth at which it must be fished and the strength of the stream dictate the tackle used. In the cold, heavy water of February to mid-April, and again, to a slightly lesser extent, in October and November, a heavy sinking line is needed to push out the big, heavy, air-resistant fly and cast it 22.8 m (25 yd) or more, and to take it down to fish deep in the flow. Number 9, 10 and 11 double-taper lines are customary for this style of fishing and to cast them, and the fly, and to be able to control them in the water and lift them off again for the next cast, a very powerful, long rod is necessary. Even on comparatively small rivers – averaging perhaps 22.8 m (25 yd) across – a 4.25 m (14 ft) rod and a line of at least size 9 would be chosen. On bigger rivers with strong flows, like the Tay or Spey, the line might need to be size 11 and the rod 5.1 m (17 ft) long.

Rod length serves a number of useful purposes. In casting, using the normal overhead cast with two hands instead of one, as for trout and seatrout, the heavy line and big fly are kept well above the fisherman's head, helping to prevent nasty accidents: a 6.5 cm (3 in) fly dressed on a length of brass tube with a treble hook at its tail-end, propelled by the heavy line (the combined weight of fly and line might be nearly 60 g (2 oz)) can cause bad wounds to the head and neck on the forward cast! The high line cast by the long rod also helps keep the fly clear of vegetation, high banks or rocks behind the caster, and it also helps make special casts, such as the Spey- or roll-cast, in which the line does not pass behind the angler, much easier.

And when the line and fly is fishing round across the current, holding the long rod out over the water helps to decrease the angle of the line to the current, thereby slowing down the fly's progress, which is desirable.

A day's salmon fishing with the big sunk fly can be extremely tiring and the fewer false-casts it is necessary to make to cover the water, the less tiring the sport becomes. The long rod permits the pool to be covered from its head to its tail, should that be deemed desirable, with the minimum of effort. After the cast has been fished out and the line is hanging almost straight downstream, the rod is brought slowly back, bringing the sunken line near to the surface and shortening it, after which a roll-cast is made to raise line tip and fly to the surface, followed by the line being lifted off into a strong back-cast, followed by an immediate delivery to allow the fly to fish down again. Usually, a couple of paces downstream are taken between casts, to cover the pool in a series of sweeps.

This may be done standing on the bank or it may be done chest-deep in strongly flowing water. Spring and autumn salmon fishing with the sunk line is definitely not a sport for the meek.

At the other extreme, with the river at low summer level, clear and at maybe 14°C (58°F) or more, the rod used might be a 2.75 m (9 ft) trout rod with a double-taper size 6 floating line and a size 10 single-hooked fly, a size 12 double or a tubefly less than 12 mm ($\frac{1}{2}$ in) long on a 2.7 kg (6 lb) leader tippet. Often, the fish will take nothing bigger in such conditions, although, for reasons of better line control – and thus fly control, since the fly only does what the line does first – many fishermen still use a double-handed rod of 3.65–4.25 m (12–14 ft) in length, even with a size 6 or 7 line. Again, water coverage with the long rod is usually carried out better and with less effort than with the trout-type rod, which entails false-casting, line-shooting and the inability to control the line on the water so well.

Rod length and weight must, of course, be selected by the fisherman to suit his physical abilities. Casting a very long rod and holding it out over the river can cause a great deal of strain on the arms, shoulders and back muscles. A big, strong man may find a 5.10 m (17 ft) graphite rod just the job, whereas a smaller man, or a boy, or a woman, might find a 3.95 m (13 ft) about as much as he or she can cope with. Good graphite rods are superb to fish with, being light and responsive. They are also very expensive – between £150 and well over £200! Good hollow-glass salmon rods from 3.65 m to 4.55 m (12–15 ft) are very good, although they are not so light as graphite and have other dis-

A spliced joint on a Sharpes bamboo salmon flyrod with the wooden protector lashed in place (top), and a joined splice secured with tape (below).

advantages. One of these is the fact that the rod needs to be fairly thick in section, and this creates wind resistance when casting, adding to the required effort, and when a wind is blowing up or down the river, even holding the rod out against wind pressure can be exhausting.

Split-bamboo rods, specially the ones where the sections are joined by splicing rather than by metal ferrules, such as those made by Farlow-Sharpe, are still popular and fish very well indeed. Up to 4.25 m (14 ft), they are manageable by any reasonably strong person, provided an occasional rest is taken after fishing a pool, and the splices do not tend to loosen and turn, causing misalignment of the rings, as metal ferrules do during the twisting stresses involved in roll-casting, and so on.

Good glass rods around 4.25 m (14 ft) cost about £30 minimum up to about £65.00. Cane rods of similar length are priced between about £100 and £130 at the time of writing.

Of course, the best way to get a suitable rod is to build it yourself from blanks, of graphite, glass or cane, depending on your purse, preferences and how much use the rod will be put to. For the occasional salmon flyfisher, a good glass rod is probably the best investment, and for sunk-line fishing and summer fishing, a happy medium would be 2.93–4.25 m (13–14 ft) for a size 9 line.

Ideally, though, I would suggest two rods: a 4.55 m (15 ft) for a size 10 or 11 line, for sunk-line work, and a 3.95–4.25 m (13–14 ft) one for a size 7 or 8 line for late spring and summer fishing. If most of your fishing is to be done in small spate rivers with floating and sink-tip lines in summer, then a 3.05 m (10 ft) rod for a size 7 line would be ideal, and could double for seatrout and for still-water trouting.

Salmon are very strong fish and even a fish of 3.6 kg (8 lb) can take the whole line and 55 m (60 yd) or more of backing from the reel in a strong downstream run in fast water. Therefore, with the thickness of heavy lines, plus the need for at least 90 m (100 yd) of 9–11.3 kg (20–25 lb) test braided Terylene backing, a reel to hold it comfortably so that, even when it has been wound on hurriedly without being neatly spread across the spool, the level of the line will be clear of the reel's crossbars and not cause jams, is necessary. Most salmon flyreels have a diameter of at least 10 cm (4 in), maybe 11.5 cm (4½ in), although some, with wide spools, may have a diameter of 9 cm (3½ in).

Reels should have good, strong checkwork and, preferably, some form of adjustment on the strength of the check or drag. Hardy's disc-dragged 'Husky' is silent – it has no audible ratchet – but yields line very smoothly. A jerky check or drag will cause lost fish by leader breakage or hook failure. Hardy's 'Marquis' salmon reels are also good, and the cheaper Shakespeare 'Beaulites' are also good, now that early problems with soft check pawls have been overcome.

A word or two more on rods is appropriate here. I believe the handles of most commercially built rods are far too long, causing uncomfortable hand positions to be made and adding unnecessary weight and bulk on the rod. I find most fishermen hold the handle with the uppermost hand well down the handle of most shop rods. Mine have a total cork length of 50 cm (20 in), which I find totally adequate, both for casting and playing fish. Some shop rods have the cork extending 76 cm (30 in) up the rod, which is unnecessary.

Whether you choose bridge rings or snakes, make sure they are hard-chromed for abrasion resistance. Tip and butt rings should be strong and of tungsten-carbide, hard-chromed steel or lined with aluminium oxide (Fuji). I would advise against intermediate Fuji single-leg rings; they are not strong enough for salmon rods.

One reel with two spare spools can hold sinking, sink-tip and floating lines, although I prefer a small reel for use in late spring and summer with the lighter lines. Balanced tackle is important.

Depending on whether the river or rivers you will fish are broad or narrow, you will need either thigh-height or chest-high waders. On slippery, rocky riverbeds felt soles are said to be best for a secure foothold, but sharp tungsten-carbide steel hobs are also good. The best chest waders, both for long life and comfort over a long day or week's fishing, are thin latex ones, worn with separate boots of oiled leather. A pair of thick woollen stockings over the feet, before the waders are put on, are necessary, plus another pair of old ones, which may be of wool or man-made fibre, over the waders, to prevent chafing the waders.

Wading brogues are expensive and a much cheaper alternative is a pair of excellent oiled-leather boots with heavy cleated rubber composition soles (such as 'Getta Grip' in the UK). Leather boots must be well dressed with neatsfoot oil and dubbin, to preserve them and keep them soft. They have the advantage of supporting the vulnerable ankle joints in the event of a trip or fall on rocky beds, or when a foot is trapped in silt or mud.

It is easy to trip, slip or become the victim of heavy current pressure when wading a powerful salmon river and a wading staff is essential for support. It is easy to make one from a well seasoned hazel staff about 1.5 cm (5 ft) long and nearly 2.5 cm (1 in) thick, drilling a hole at the top (thinner) end for a lanyard attachment to belt or shoulder strap, and wrapping sheet lead, to keep the end down in fast water, round the base and nailing it with brass or copper nails. The lower end may have a metal spike, or a walking-stick or crutch rubber on it; rubber being best. It is surprising how much more difficult wading in deep, fast water, to cover extra lies, can be done with the confidence instilled by a staff, used on the fisherman's downstream side.

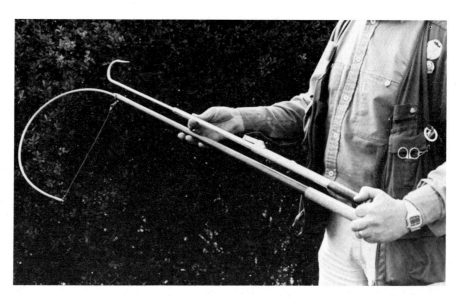

A collapsible gaff (top) and a tailer – two methods of securing a beaten salmon.

Salmon may be landed by hand-tailing, getting a good grip round the firm wrist of the fish's tail with the thumb and forefinger towards the tail, but this is only possible where the fish can be played out and picked up from shallow, slack water. Doing so while holding up a long flyrod is no easy task, and a partner is the best answer. Salmon can also be beached, but again, this depends on whether the river has suitable, shallow sloping spots, which some do not.

The single-handed salmon fisherman is better off with a gaff or a tailer. The gaff is easier to use, and the hook is placed over the beaten fish's back while it lies tired, head to current, and then pulled home and the fish lifted in one smooth movement. However, there is something a bit brutal about gaffing such a beautiful fish, and many fishermen now eschew the gaff. In any event, the gaffed fish should be killed immediately it is safely on the bank, using a suitable priest over the eyes. All fish intended for the pot should be humanely killed in this way with the minimum time-lapse between water and dry land.

The gaff may be a hook with a 7.5 cm (3 in) gape and tang securely lashed to a 1.3–1.5 m (4–5 ft) hazel or ash pole and slung over the back on a cord, or one of the extending models, which are about 90 cm (3 ft) long when opened and less than half that when closed. They are worn clipped to belt or a lanyard ring on a shoulder harness, so that they hang between the shoulder-blades out of the way when fishing.

Leaders for salmon fishing need not usually be tapered: a length of level nylon cut straight from a spool is normally sufficient, and 3.5 kg (8 lb) test is about right for most fishing in the April–September period, with 5.5–6.7 kg (12–15 lb) for sunk-line work with big flies. On rare occasions in summer, when the river runs very low and gin clear and when size 12 doubles or single-hook flies down to size 10, or a 12 mm ($\frac{1}{2}$ in) tubefly with a size 14 treble hook, may be the only sure way of attracting takes, a knotless-tapered leader to about 2.7 kg (6 lb) test might be an advantage, not only for delicate presentation but to permit the nylon to pass easily through the tiny hook eyes.

Most other items used for salmon flyfishing are the same as those required for trout fishing: scissors, artery forceps, hook-sharpening stone, leader-sinking compound, polarizing spectacles, and so on. In addition, some form of carrier for toting the fish along the bank is required, since carrying a salmon of even 4.5 kg (10 lb) is quite a chore, due to the length of the fish, let alone its weight. What is needed is a wooden or plastic handle and some cord through its centre, with a loop to go round the tail of the fish and a big hook to fix in the gills or head region, so the fish is carried slung rather than with head or tail trailing along the ground.

Because, when fishing down salmon pools, it is often necessary to wade in through a gap in a tree-lined bank at the top of the pool, and then fish down it by wading, without being able to emerge until the tail of the pool is reached, due either to a heavily-treed bank, a steep, high bank, or perhaps a deep-water channel alongside the bank, it can be seen that any spare tackle items must be carried by the fisherman. Again, the best way to do this is to wear a flyfisher's waistcoat with the flyboxes, spare nylon, priest, etc., carried in the many pockets. A word of warning here: if you will need to wade above waist height for much of your fishing, make sure the waistcoat you choose is a short one intended for use with chest waders. Longer ones will reach the water and the contents will get soaked!

One important item I have not yet mentioned is the thermometer for taking water temperature. There are tables of temperature ranges for use as a guide to the size of fly needed, and even to its pattern, but the best way to use a thermometer is to take the temperature of the pool after each fish is caught, noting time of day, weather conditions, fly pattern and size, and any other information thought relevant. After a while, a pattern will emerge and this can be a very useful source of reference as the information builds up over the years.

Gaining access to salmon fishing

Finally, before we discuss flyfishing techniques, it must be said that the charges made for salmon fishing vary tremendously and that, usually, the more you can afford to pay, the better the fishing. Five hundred to a thousand pounds a week may be charged for good fishing at the best times of the season, but much fishing is controlled by hotels, who offer a package deal of fishing with accommodation, many of these being excellent value. Clubs and associations often offer membership at a reasonable fee on a temporary basis, and some salmon fishing is available by the day permit. Good hotel fishing may be had for about £70 per week, not including accommodation, of course, but I have caught four salmon in a day – and lost two others – on water available at £8 per day!

Great slews of salmon are made on the expensive beats at the best times, but having done that once or twice, it becomes a little sickening to kill so many fine fish. It is far more satisfying to have to fish well and hard for a fish a day – or even over two days. Just so long as there are fish in the river, with at least a few fresh-run ones, then fishing can be interesting and worthwhile. On some small spate streams, which fish well only just after heavy rainfall, as the

The author fishes for salmon on the lovely little River Dwyfawr in North Wales, guided by the late Jack Owen, who knew the river like the back of his hand.

river begins to fall, the cost of a day may well be only £1–2, but arriving at the best time can be more by luck than by judgement.

And a word of caution. Always try to establish before you go to a river if it is fly-only, or if it is fly-only during certain levels of water flow. Trying to fish the fly successfully on pools being raked by anglers spinning, worm fishing and prawn fishing, is rather a waste of time – and very galling to the flyfisher!

Flyfishing disturbs the water and fish very little if done reasonably well, and even on hard-fished association and hotel beats, each fisherman has a chance as he follows his predecessor down the pool in rotation, which is as it should be – you never enter below another angler on a salmon pool; you go in above him after he has fished down at least 22.8 m (25 yd), and then follow him down, keeping at about that distance. And keep moving; it is considered bad manners to remain in one place for too long.

But when spinning is going on, the salmon see the big, flashy baits too often and the illusion that makes them take is usually impossible to achieve with a fly – although sometimes a fly following a spinner catches the fish. Over-crowded hotel and association waters are terrible places to fish with the fly.

A classic case of ruined salmon rivers is found on many of the Welsh rivers, beautiful fisheries but overcrowded and overfished by those who think of salmon only in terms of the cash made by selling them.

Salmon fishing should be confined to fly only, from 1 April until 30 September, with perhaps some spinning and bait fishing being permitted between those times when the water level is very high, although, with few exceptions, it is possible to catch salmon on a big fly and sunk line as well as they are taken on a spinner, when the water is high and carrying extra colour. The reason for this is that a salmon has to be in a taking mood to accept a fly, whereas a fish may be harried with worms, prawns and even spinners when spotted in a pool, until it takes the lure or bait out of sheer annoyance; and sometimes, these fish are deliberately foul-hooked. In addition, a salmon fishery can carry more flyfishing rods than bait rods without being overfished, and can still produce sufficient sport, without depleting unnecessarily the already decreasing stocks of salmon in our rivers.

Flyfishing only is permitted in North American and Canadian rivers for Atlantic salmon, as a conservation exercise. Why not elsewhere?

Much of the greed and poor sportsmanship would be removed from salmon fishing – and maybe the cost could be lowered, too – if each fisherman were to be limited to catching four fish a day, or perhaps the limit bag could be varied to suit the river. Some fisheries already enforce a bag limit and I have yet to hear a complaint where this is so.

There are rivers where a fisherman can catch forty salmon in five days fishing and when the fish is fetching £2.00 for 450 g (1 lb), the fish become more important than the fishing. That's £800 in the man's pocket – and even if his hotel and fishing bill came to £400, he has made a very large profit. That should not be what salmon fishing is all about.

Chapter Nine

Going fishing: the salmon season

The basis of salmon fishing with the fly is a very simple one. It is to cast the flyline across and slightly downstream of one's position, and allow it to swing across the flow fairly slowly, with the fly on its almost invisible leader following it, sinking and lifting, fluttering its delicate dressing of feather-fibres and hairs in the vagaries of the current as it does so. That the fly may fish within 2.5 cm (1 in) or so of the surface or within 30 cm (1 ft) or so of the riverbed is simply a variation in level.

This action of the fly, be it a big, colourful fly in cold, powerful water in February or March, or a tiny drab one on a hot July day, is attractive to the salmon, which swims up to intercept its movement and take it. Usually a salmon takes a fly very deliberately, holding it in its mouth and returning from whence it came – to its lie. In most cases, striking at the take of a salmon as one does to a trout taking a nymph or wet fly, is incorrect.

With a sunk line in cold water the take is usually felt as a sudden strong pull and the instinctive reaction is to pull back. And this is correct in this case, since the fly has been taken deep, or fairly so, in the water, and usually with a fair length of line out, which is how the fly fishes most deeply, dragged down by the heavy sinking line. And the line will usually have a bow in it as it swings across the stream, which is partially straightened by the pull of the fish as it takes the fly and swings back to its lie. All this takes time, albeit only a second or less, and it is enough for a simple firm lifting of the rod, preferably sideways and up rather than in a perpendicular direction, away from the direction of the pull, to sink the barb in the side of the salmon's jaw.

One hears advice to let the salmon take line from the reel before tightening, but few fishermen can control their reactions in the excitement of the moment, should the truth be known. One also hears of holding about 90 cm (1 yd) of slack line between reel and butt ring, letting it go when the pull is felt before lifting the rod. But a loop of line in such a place is often the cause of tangles, and I have had no problem with hooking fish on the sunk line and big fly by doing as I have advised. I lift and hold the line firmly against the cork handle with the upper hand as I do so.

Fishing in warmer water and weather conditions, with the floating or sink-tip line and with the fly fishing 2.5 cm (1 in) subsurface, or maybe as deep as

Watched by his son, the author regains line on a salmon that had just moved upstream again after taking nearly 90 m (100 yd) of line from his reel on the Blackwater in Ireland. The fish took a small Roe Purple in fast water. The rod is a 4.2 m (14 ft) Diamondback.

30 cm (1 ft) in slower water, the situation at the take is quite different. Often, the fish is seen to come to the fly, head and back breaking surface as it takes, before it goes down again. Or the boil of the fish taking a little deeper will be seen, and the line will suddenly tighten.

It is tempting to strike immediately, and this is wrong, because the line that is floating, or mainly lying on the surface, transmits to the angler what is happening at the fly end of his tackle much more quickly than when the line is deep in the water, bellying downstream, and the fish invisible. And in any case, in summer conditions, the angler will try to control his floating line so that no downstream belly – or excessive belly at any rate – forms, dragging his fly across the stream more quickly than is usually desirable. The floating line can be *mended*, lifted upstream by a slow, circular movement of the rod, both immediately after the cast has been made and during the line's travel across the river. This avoids the fast current that often flows between the angler and where his fly is fishing, dragging the intermediate line downstream faster than the tip.

Mending floating line to
slow down the passage of
the fly across the flow
A-B Line of cast.
A-C Current drags line in
     mid-river; fly's speed
     increases.
A-D Line is mended
     upstream, slowing
     fly's progress.
A-E Fly fishes at right
     speed for fish.

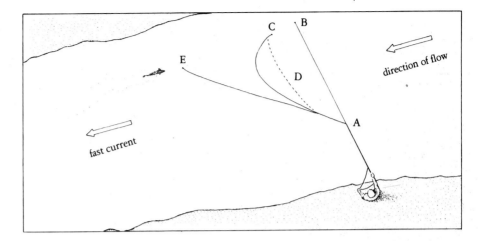

A sunken line cannot be thus controlled, although it often pays to mend the
line immediately the cast has been made and before the line has been able to
sink very far, to allow the line to gain depth before the intervening current
gets hold of it.

So, with the fly high in the water and the floating/sink-tip line, a degree of
delay in tightening is desirable. It permits the fish time to take the fly, close its
mouth, and begin to turn away and down to its lie again. A pull by the fisherman at that moment, with the fish facing away from him and maybe turning
its head downstream, will pull the hook *back* into the jaw. An early tightening
may pull the fly out of the salmon's mouth before the mouth has closed, or
even if it has closed, a pull from directly or slightly upstream can pull the fly
forward and out of the mouth.

For these reasons, then, a take on the fly being fished high in the water
should be delayed, and the metre of line between reel and butt ring serves to
make this possible. The line is let go until it tightens, and then the answering
pull is given.

Some fishermen are incapable of such self-control and for them it is best to
fish with the reel on a light drag or check tension, and without holding the
line at all. When the take comes, he must wait until he hears the line begin to
leave the reel, and only then should he tighten up.

I said at the outset of this chapter that the basis of flyfishing for salmon was
a simple one – which it is – although it may seem to be getting more complicated as I go along. For there are occasions when, instead of trying to avoid a
belly in the floating line – and thus fishing the fly too quickly across a fast
current – the fisherman either tries to create a slight downstream belly or
actually strips line in with his free hand, rather like fishing a reservoir fly or
lure, to make the fly fish faster.

Such instances occur when fishing slow water in which salmon are known
to be lying but in which more life than the current will give is needed to fish
the fly in an attractive manner. Remember, the salmon was chasing his food
in the sea and it is the moving object that attracts him. A fly simply drifting
lifelessly down the river is very unlikely to attract a fish.

You will read in some books, and hear from some fishermen, of a technique called 'greased-line fishing'. They will tell you that the fly must not move across the current in this technique but that the floating line must be constantly mended, so that the fly 'drifts down like a dead thing'. They are quoting the words of Arthur Wood, who lived on Deeside in Scotland and who invented greased-line fishing at a time when the only way to make a salmon flyline – then made of silk – float was to grease it.

Well, the modern plastic floating line has made the term 'greased line' obsolete, and those writers who have since said the fly must not drag, but just drift down the current, were and are talking utter nonsense. I doubt whether the late Mr Wood intended that term to be used to describe his way of fishing, and even if he did, he was wrong, too.

It does not take an honours degree in physics to know that a fly drifting downstream without dragging will go on drifting on the same path for as long as the river flows; it cannot cross to the angler's side of the river, unless brought there by a change in the current's direction. I believe that what Wood was so insistent upon was that the fly should not be dragged at great speed across the river by the current bellying the line downstream. He thus made a great play upon line-mending.

Today, far too many fishermen mend line far too often, and frequently for no good reason. On most salmon pools the line may be cast at such an angle that, apart from an immediate mend, to allow the fly to sink a little before the line begins to drag it across, no mending at all is necessary as the fly comes across. Holding the long rod out over the water, and with its tip high, to keep as much of the line near the angler as possible off any faster water than that in which the fly is fishing, helps to fish the fly across slowly, as I have mentioned earlier.

When stripping the fly to give it life as it slowly crosses slow-moving water, the take is likely to be very similar to that of a still-water trout on a lure: a sudden hard pull. And since the fisherman is pulling line, too, the hook is likely to penetrate the fish's jaw at the instant it takes – or it will not get a hold at all. I always lift firmly immediately I feel the fish pull, and find no better solution. Some takes will always be missed, whatever method is used, either due to an incorrect reaction by the fisherman, or because the fish miscalculated its interception of the fly, only touching it or missing it completely, or even 'bunting' the fly with its mouth closed.

The best way to learn salmon flyfishing is to go fishing with somebody who has experience, beginning in the cold months of the salmon-fisher's so-called spring, progressing through the true spring, through the hot summer and finishing in the autumn. So be my guest for a few days in March on a river with a good spring run, a river with varied salmon water, both the fast, streamy water running through rocky terrain, interspersed with deep, slow-flowing reaches.

Early spring

We arrive at 9.00 am on our hotel beat for the day to find the river running high but fairly clear, with just a hint of amber from the run-off coming down from rain on the peaty moorland of the headwaters. It's a dull morning, chill and with a strongish wind blowing slightly downstream and into our bank – the water temperature shows 8°C (47°F) and it is unlikely we shall see any fish showing on the surface, even though fresh ones are known to be creeping up, since we are only twelve miles from the sea.

The river here averages about 27.4 m (30 yd) in width, with some fast, narrow stretches only 18.3 m (20 yd) between rocky walls, and some pools 36.5 m (40 yd) wide. All these factors make me put up the 4.25 m (14 ft) graphite rod and a number 10 DT sinking line – a medium-fast sinker, since the river is rarely more than 2.4 m (8 ft) deep on this beat, which is nearly a mile long.

A 2.7 m (9 ft) length of 6.5 kg (14 lb) test nylon is cut from a spool and tied with a grinner knot to the tiny loop whipped to hold the doubled line-core securely. We open the flyboxes and enjoy poring over the rows of single-hook spring flies on hooks from 1 to 4/0 in one box, and the hair-wing tube-flies in the other box. Because the water is high with that touch of beer-colour, and because I have confidence in the hooking ability of trebles, I select a 5 cm (2 in) tube of hard nylon with a 'wing' of mixed primrose-yellow and orange bucktail hairs and a body on which the front half is of bright yellow silk and the rear half of black silk, the whole ribbed with broad silver tinsel, for flash in the water. I slide the tube up the leader and tie on a size 10 strong treble hook which last night I sharpened with a small abrasive stone. Having tied the grinner, I slide the tube back down the nylon and push the eye of the hook firmly into the 9 mm ($\frac{3}{8}$ in) of soft plastic tubing whipped to the back-end of the tube. This was whipped on securely before the body dressing was applied. It holds the hook firmly; without it the treble would let the tube slide up the leader, causing tangles when casting. With the tube holding it, the hook is always in a good position to hook a taking fish.

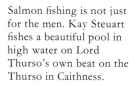

Salmon fishing is not just for the men. Kay Steuart fishes a beautiful pool in high water on Lord Thurso's own beat on the Thurso in Caithness.

Our top pool this day is a very attractive one, and the gillie at the hotel told us this morning over a post-breakfast chat that it should produce a fish. He has also marked our sketch-map of the beat with some crosses to show other likely spots with the river at this height. The water comes rushing down through a rocky ravine and spreads out, the main flow being deflected towards the far bank by a bank projection on our side. The fast and turbulent water at the head of the pool is unlikely to hold fish now, although in low water in summer, it will be well stocked, most likely. Today the fish should be lying in the deeper, smoother-flowing water on the edge of the main current, just below where the underwater rocks cause whirls to show on the surface, and then on down towards the smooth, shallower tail of the pool where the bottom is shale and gravel.

I would begin fishing some half-way down the pool, not wading unless I had to, to cover the good-looking water. Line is stripped from the reel – enough to let me cast the 18.3 m (20 yd) or so to cover the river at this point – and dropped on the ground at my feet. I then work out line, and drop the fly some 1.8 m (6 ft) from the far bank and laying the line down at an angle of about 45° downstream – this means a cast midway between straight across the river from my position and the line of the bank on my downstream side. I make an upstream mend quickly, before the line begins to sink, and then hold the rod out over the river at an angle of about 20° to the water surface and pointing a little downstream.

The line sinks and the current begins to swing it across, the fly following. I do not follow round with the rod. I keep it well out over the river, narrowing the angle of the line to the flow, and so slowing down the progress of the fly across the river. Nothing happens, so, when the line is immediately downstream of my position, I strip in a few metres of line, slowly, then lift the rod high, roll-cast to lift the sunken line to the surface, then lift off into a strong back-cast, stop the rod, allow the line to straighten high on the back-cast, then make another delivery at the same angle and distance.

Again nothing. I take two paces downstream and repeat the exercise, taking another two paces each time I re-cast. This systematically covers the river in a

Sunk-line fishing, showing how the fly fishes over a rock on slow-to-medium sinking line

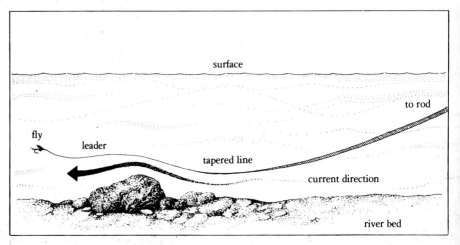

surface

to rod

fly

leader

tapered line

current direction

river bed

Top: Left column, top to bottom: Damselfly Nymph number 1, Damselfly Nymph number 2, Sedge Pupa number 3, Sedge Pupa number 1, Sedge Pupa number 2; *middle column, top to bottom:* Sedge Larva number 1, Sedge Larva number 3, Sedge Larva number 2, Pond Olive Nymph, Pheasant Tail Nymph, Claret Nymph, Shrimp; *right column, top to bottom:* Black Midge Pupa, Red Midge Pupa, Pale Green Midge Pupa, Olive Midge Pupa, Golden Dun Midge Pupa, Orange/Silver Midge Pupa, Phantom Midge Pupa, Fluorescent Red Midge Pupa, Fluorescent Green Midge Pupa.

Middle: Top left, Dry Fly number 1, *bottom left,* Dry Fly number 4, *centre,* Black and Peacock Spider Variant, *top right,* Dry Fly number 2, *bottom right,* Dry Fly number 3.

Bottom: Top left, Vulture (Matuka style), *middle left,* Esox-it (pike fly), *bottom left,* estuary seatrout lure; *top right,* Black Marabou, *middle right,* White Marabou, *bottom right,* estuary seatrout lure.

series of fan-like paths, thus showing the fly to any salmon lying in the pool at close range, so they do not have to move far or fast to take the fly.

I like a lightish fly in most conditions, except where the flow is very fast and the water very deep, in which case a heavier fly, perhaps a tube with a brass body over the nylon tubing, would get down better. But I like the *line* to take the fly down, and then the fly can be lifted by the pressures of the current and eddies, rising over rocks to follow the line, then falling again on the downstream side. This covers deep-lying salmon in cold water well and prevents undue snagging of the fly on rocks and other riverbed projections.

Never be in a hurry when salmon fishing in cold spring conditions unless you see a fish show at the tail of the pool as you are fishing down. And then get to that fish as quickly as you can, to show him your fly. A fish that shows as a silvery arc is an almost certain taker if you can cover him. Otherwise, fish down the pool calmly, concentrating on getting your fly to fish deep and slow across the river, using as little effort as possible, but as much of the rod's flexibility instead, to do your casting for you. A tired salmon fisherman is a poor fisherman and in spring salmon fishing, it is the man who keeps going the longest who normally brings home the best catch.

Certainly, skill is demanded: to decide where fish might be resting; to fish the right fly at the right depth and the right speed; to play and secure the fish. However, in the long run, persistence is the real key to salmon-fishing success; that, and an eye for the water.

There is no way I can put words on this page that will tell you how to learn to read salmon water. That, like many things in country sports, must come with time and observation.

Try to get your mind to wriggle its way down the line to your sunken fly as you fish. Imagine what the fly is doing, and what any salmon may be doing, too. Deep and slow is the spring fisherman's code, and if you need to wade out to fish the fly more slowly over a particular spot, then do it. Take trouble; take time. Fish every metre of the water; if you come to trees lining your bank, do not walk around them just because casting will be a problem. If possible – and this goes for a high bank behind, or a cliff, too – wade in and roll-cast your way past the hazard behind. Others may have taken the easy way out and left a fish there for you.

Do not follow flyfishing lore slavishly. If you have an idea, try it. I once decided to fish in a rising spate with yellow and orange tube-flies 2.5 cm (1 in) long instead of the customary 5 cm (2 in) or 7.5 cm (3 in) flies. I caught more fish than the others fishing the river. I cannot say why, but I did have confidence in what I was doing, mainly because the larger flies had failed me and the others.

Although spring salmon tend to lie in the deeper, slower water half-way down the pool and towards the tail, rather than face the energy-sapping turmoil in the head of the pool, they will sometimes lie in very shallow gliding water only 90 cm (3 ft) deep. Such water is usually found near the tails of pools, where the gravel bed is clean and firm, causing no surface turmoil. And always fish your fly right round to your own bank, or to a point immediately below your position when wading. And even then, draw the fly up towards you by stripping line slowly by hand before roll-casting and lifting off for the next cast. Salmon often follow the fly in, and if you lift it away from them prematurely you will never know.

If you get a quick snatch, or see a fish boil at your fly, or have any suspicion at all that a fish tried to take, reel in, walk back upstream 1.8–2.7 m (2–3 yd), then fish down to the same spot again. The chances are that the fish will take you properly next time down. If not, try a fly 12 mm ($\frac{1}{2}$ in) smaller, and if that fails, rest the spot for ten minutes and then try a fly 12 mm ($\frac{1}{2}$ in) longer than the original pattern.

I do not believe that, in spring fishing, changing the pattern of the fly makes very much difference. I rate only the orange/yellow/black combination for cloudy, high water, although an alternative on a bright day with high but clear water conditions is a fly with a mixed black and turquoise hair wing and a silver-ribbed black body.

Not all early spring fishing comes with high, cloudy water, and when rivers are low, clear and cold, a fly 3.8 cm ($1\frac{1}{2}$ in) long might create the desired illusion. I never fish the traditional single-hook flies with their multitude of vari-coloured materials because I do not believe the fish can tell the difference between those complicated dressings and the more basically-coloured simple ones dressed on tubes or Waddington mounts. A Waddington mount is a length of strong steel wire, on which the fly is dressed, with an eye at one end to attach to the leader and an eye or clip at the other, to take a treble hook. Why do I like treble-hooked flies for spring fishing? Because they hook well and, if as so often happens, a hook point is broken or blunted, the treble may be replaced. On a single hook, a broken hook makes the fly fit only for dumping. And big, thick, traditional-style hooks are not very good hookers of fish.

Once a fish is hooked, play it from the reel. Keep the rod high, well bent and move around to keep abreast or slightly downstream of your fish. Stay upstream when a fish runs down, and when you put strain on him again you will be pulling the hook towards the front of the fish's mouth – and maybe out of it. Keep as much of the heavy flyline as possible out of the water. The drag of the line can break the leader if the fish moves fast enough to create a big bow in the sunken line.

Fish for as long as you are able. Pace yourself throughout the day. Although the optimum taking time in the period from mid-February to mid-April is generally around 11.00 am until about 2.30 pm (when the water should be at its warmest), a fish will often take just as the light is failing.

Changes in the weather pattern during a day can make fish take. For instance, on a dull, cold drizzly morning, a fifteen-minute spell of sunshine can be the only time in the day that a fish will take. Sometimes a change in wind direction, especially from north or east (the worst wind) to south or west, will bring fish on the take – and if you are sitting in the car drinking whisky or hot soup you will not catch a fish.

The advice of a local fisherman or gillie *before* going fishing can be priceless, but many people then like to fish alone, trying the suggested places with the suggested methods, but then changing methods and trying other places if the initial attempts fail. However, on some big rivers with spring runs, fishing is often done from boats handled by gillies, and they can be very fixed in their ways; having an 'expert' looking over your shoulder uttering a series of admonishments as you experiment is extremely inhibiting.

I shall never forget a week on the Thurso at the beginning of a cold May. The river was in good order for our first day and I caught two fish, but gales and torrential rain that day and for most of the week raised the water level by more than a metre: inimical to flyfishing success. We flogged on and the friend sharing my beats, Richard Ogden, actually took a fresh-run fish when the river had risen some 1.2 m (4 ft), and all the other rods at the hotel had given up. He took it in a spot which had been dry land the previous day – a slightly shelving shingle beach alongside a steep bank – and on a yellow tube-fly 2.5 cm (1 in) long! To 99 per cent of fishermen, that was water fit only for worming.

Early summer

By May, perhaps by mid-April in some years, water temperatures will have risen to about 10°C (50°F), or maybe a little more, and the water will also be running at a lower level and often quite clear. Fish are now more active, being able to see the fly more clearly from a distance of maybe 6 m (20 ft), though usually less than half that, and are prepared to move to intercept, or even chase the fly across the river.

Because the river is lower, fish may be more inclined to lie nearer the heads of the pools, although the tails (where the water is 90 cm (1 yd) deep or more) will still be tenanted. This can be a time of fluctuating conditions and fluctuating sport.

If the water is clear and at a moderate height, and around 10°C (50°F) or more, a floating or sink-tip line and a low-water fly size 6, or a tube or Waddington about 19 mm ($\frac{3}{4}$ in) long may be just what the fish want. And they may want it within 7.5 cm (3 in) of the surface. However, night frosts can occur even in May, and although the water is low, a very cold river may call for a return to the sunk line with a fly 5 cm (2 in) long.

Fishing the floating or sink-tip line and a smaller fly near the surface is much more enjoyable than the early-season sunk-line technique. One is more in contact with the fly, the line may be controlled by mending – although this should not be done excessively, since it can cause too much disturbance of the surface and alarm fish in shallow water – and the fish that come to the fly may often be seen to do so. In addition, the rod and line are lighter and more delicate to handle.

The fly may be fished in many different ways to be effective. It may be attractive to the fish coming back quite quickly, having been cast almost straight across the flow. Or it may need to be cast on a long line at a very shallow angle down and over, with mending to allow it to come across very slowly. And in smooth, slow-flowing water, the fly may be cast across and stripped back smoothly by hand. All have taken fish in this period of the year.

Fly pattern may now be more important. In the heavy, cold and coloured water of early spring, the main aim was to let the fish see the fly, and thus we chose a yellow/orange fly of reasonable size. But now, we do not want the fish to see the fly too easily: it must be seen, but only vaguely, crossing the fish's vision like a small live creature, fluttering, falling and rising again. Flies with black bodies, a black 'wing' and a blue hackle, bodies lightly ribbed with fine silver wire or tinsel, are often killing. So are flies with plain silver bodies, speckled teal flank-feather wings, or 'wings' of brown mallard flank feathers, with a black or brown hackle. An all-black fly with just a hint of silver ribbing on the body may also do well. I still often use a fly with some dull orange in its make-up, a shrimp-like pattern with jungle cock cheeks.

On one day a size 8 fly will be taken; on another a size 6, or even a size 1. You never know. Try them all.

If a day that begins warm, with sunshine and some cloud cover, changes to become cold and dull, fish the fly deeper, even with a sinking line. Again, never give up. The fly that is longest in the water stands the best chance of catching a fish.

Longer leaders are often necessary to separate the small fly from the bulk or shadow of the heavy flyline, and I recommend 3.6 or 3.9 m (12 or 13 ft) in clear water.

Now is the time to delay tightening when a fish pulls or is seen to rise to the fly. The fish sees the fly's approach for a greater distance and is able to make a leisurely interception. Let it turn down with the fly or take 90 cm (1 yd) or so of line before raising the rod firmly.

Even then you will have heartbreaks.

One May morning, I arrived to fish my beat on the Hampshire Avon below Ringwood and put up a fly I had dressed a day or so previously. It was on about a size 6 low-water hook and I had tried to make it look like a shrimp. It had jungle cock cheeks, a little orange hackle, some dyed brown squirrel hair and a body of black and orange silk. On the second cast across the tail of a pool called Lake's Ditch the fly was taken. The floating line drew tight and I delayed properly and lifted. The fish made a great swirl on the smooth water, then heaved itself clear. I had never seen such a fish before; I have never seen one so big since. It was at least 13.6 kg (30 lb) and possibly 18 kg (40 lb).

It seemed to hang there for several seconds, before falling back with a splash like a cow had fallen in. Then the line was slack. The hook was perfectly all right. I think I cried.

In April and May, salmon often like to lie in swirling, fast water where there are many rocks, and it is in such places that the fly fishes so well. A spinner or bait will become snagged, but a fly can be fished across the turmoil and hung to waver from upstream over likely spots. A light fly is best for this fast, ripply water, and often a sink-tip line will fish it better than a full floater.

True salmon rivers in normal conditions do not carry much floating or water-borne debris, and their beds are fairly open, giving the fish ample opportunity to see a fly coming to them. It is probably the first water-borne object behaving slightly unusually, in that it is not simply being carried down by the flow but is moving across it as well that they have seen all day.

However, on south country rivers, such as the Hampshire Avon, the lower Test and the Itchen, the Frome, Piddle, and so on, the beds of the rivers are rich in weed-beds, and fronds cut by keepers are often drifting down. Fish lying near the weeds have little field of vision, and a fly much larger than would be needed to make the correct impact on a Scottish or Irish river in the same clarity and height of water is needed. Where a size 8 low-water fly or a similar length tube might be ideal on the Scottish river, the Test or Avon might need a size 4 or even a 3.8 cm ($1\frac{1}{2}$ in) yellow tube-fly to get results.

Mid-summer

In June, July and August in a dry year, the water levels in the rivers will become very low, and the water will be clear. The temperature of the water itself can be as high as $18°C$ ($65°F$) and now is the time for a further change in fishing technique.

In any water temperature over about $14°C$ ($58°F$) and with the main pools almost without flow, the salmon, seeking shelter in depth and a better supply of dissolved oxygen, will tend to move to the faster, rocky or broken water. This often means that the best chance of a fish on the fly will be when using a tiny, fairly sombre fly, perhaps a size 12 double or a size 10 single low-water hook. The heads of the pools, where the water rushes from the glide out of the pool above and bubbles and forms dancing wavelets, little cross-currents, eddies and a strong V-shaped stream are the places to fish, although the tails of pools, especially rocky ones, where there is at least 60 cm (2 ft) of water, can still be productive if the fish have not been unduly disturbed.

In low water conditions, it pays not to keep flogging the available likely

Narrows on rivers are favourite lies for salmon, since the constricted flow cuts a deep channel, usually with steep sides against which the fish love to lie. Here the author hangs a fly just below such a neck, where a grilse has just shown.

water. During spells of bright, sunny and warm weather, with low water, the optimum times to expect success are early morning, before the sun is high, and again just before sundown. The best time may not last much more than an hour, and it is best to be on the water before the normal hotel breakfasting time, return for breakfast, then idle away the daylight hours with just the occasional couple of carefully made casts into the likely spots, or to cover a fish seen to move. Try to get back to the hotel, or to home, for an early dinner and be on the water again as the sun goes down. Fishing to this pattern in the conditions outlined is far more worthwhile for the short periods when fish may take, than to flog away during the day so as to fit in with hotel or family arrangements.

If you have to fish the slow water for any reason – perhaps a fish is seen to move there or fish are seen lying there with the aid of polarizing spectacles – try to present line and fly as you would when fishing for trout. Salmon do not seem to pay so much attention to anglers on the bank as trout do, and they will often continue to lie in view without showing signs of disturbance, whereas trout will be away immediately. However, just because the salmon lie there, it does not mean that they are unaware of your presence, and the likelihood of a take is very doubtful.

The aim should be to make the presentation of the fly to the fish, without it seeing angler or any part of the tackle, and at the optimum time of day – and it should be the first fly that fish has seen in that day, either at daybreak or near sunset. It is the surprise factor of the presentation in these difficult conditions that takes the fish.

Very often, little areas of streamy water in which fish tend to lie are found well out in the river – a trough with rocks at the sides, perhaps, with shallow, flat gravel on either side stretching to both banks. Careful wading to fish such spots is called for, and the fly may simply be dangled to swim from side to side in the little area of water that may be only 1.8 m (2 yd) square, making it do so by side-to-side rod tip movements.

Casting a short line to fish the fly similarly in the little roily spots at the heads of the pools is another good tactic. There is no point in making long casts just for the sake of it. Treat the salmon in these conditions as wary trout and your success rate will increase. Mend line as little as possible on low, clear rivers; instead, concentrate on placing the line at the correct angle in the delivery. Line mending on a low, clear river with strong overhead light is the best way I know of ruining chances.

Fishing with perhaps only 3.6 m (12 ft) of line plus the leader outside the tip ring like this calls for gentle casting movements. There is insufficient weight in that length of line to work the long rod, but care will get it moving all right. Hold the rod tip high, to keep as much line off the surface as possible. If the pocket of rough water is broad rather than a long, narrow gully, then try a cast almost straight across at first, and do not mend. Let the fly fish across fast, just below the surface or even skating a little. This can be very effective and the fish that do take usually come with a rush.

In rivers with big grilse runs – fish of maybe 1.8–3.6 kg (4–8 lb) – at this period of the season, sport can be excellent provided light tackle and small flies are used, to give the fish a chance to show their paces. These small, silvery salmon will lie in very shallow broken runs, maybe only 60 cm (2 ft) deep, even less, provided they are not flogged. Grilse seem more active than the other larger summer salmon and will chase a small fly that has been cast square across the flow and allowed to cross the stream quickly. It may pay, in gliding water where grilse are lying, to strip the fly back, 90 cm (1 yd) of line being taken in at a time.

In small rivers – say, less than 27.4 m (30 yd) in width – or in broad rivers that have shrunk, due to the low water, to a series of runs between areas of flat, shallow water – grilse fishing is best done with an easy-action trout rod of 2.75–3.20 m (9–10½ ft) and a double-taper floating or sink-tip line size 5–6. The small flies used will be perfectly well fished on this light line and the delicate presentation achieved is a great advantage. And because grilse tend to prefer a fly that fishes quite quickly across the fast, streamy runs, the short rod is no disadvantage. The use of the long rod to hold out the line and fish the fly slowly is now of little account.

Many of the normal winged trout and seatrout wet flies will take grilse better than small standard salmon flies, and even the tiny (size 14) hackled North Country spider-type trout flies have accounted for plenty of grilse. Some of the still-water trout flies with slim hair wings – such as the Sweeney Todd and the Church Fry – are excellent, too, for grilse.

Autumn

In some years, September sees a quick cooling of the water, and sometimes the autumn rains begin. By mid-October, late summer-run salmon may still be entering the river, with some grilse, too, and the first of the big autumn fish. With such a variety of fish in the river, and with changing weather conditions – from Indian summer to the first touches of frost – methods must vary too.

In addition, another factor presents itself, especially on rivers running through well-wooded country. Dead leaves begin to drift down and the salmon, seeing all these objects, become bored and may not bother to investigate a small fly that looks similar to all those objects drifting by. It may be that a bright, 3.8–5 cm (1½–2 in) fly, fairly garish in dressing, and moving differently to the leaves – hesitantly darting across the current – will be just what the fish is waiting for.

In this transitional period between summer and autumn, then, tactics must be varied with the conditions. For two days the size 10 or 8 low-water fly fly fished just subsurface may work and then, with a period of rainfall and colder conditions, a sunk line with a 3.8 cm (1½ in) tube or a double-hook shrimp pattern may be best.

True autumn salmon fishing on such rivers as the Tweed (upper), Tay, Nith, the Esks and Wales' Dovey, Mawddach, and England's Lune and Ribble, for example, often demands a return to sunk-line fishing with big showy flies, as is done in the 'spring'. As the water cools in October and even into November on some of the rivers that remain open later, the fish will tend to lie in the deeper water of the pools again, and want a big fly fished slowly past their noses.

And so we have fished through the salmon season on the rivers.

Tweed in Peebleshire. Salmon fishing is not very good in this area until autumn, although a few fish may be taken in late spring and summer. The fly is being fished under the trees where the water is deeper.

Still-water salmon fishing

I have not mentioned flyfishing for salmon in the loughs of Ireland or the lochs of Scotland, from a boat. Essentially, this is a summer-time sport, usually best from June onwards, and is pursued rather like seatrout fishing on the same waters. Its success depends largely upon the local knowledge of the boatman, who must be able to put the fisherman over the best areas in the varying conditions. The main difference between it and seatrout fishing on the big lakes is that the fly must be fished closer to the surface. The dibbled dropper works well, as for seatrout, and both casting downwind from a drifting boat and casting from the side of a boat being rowed slowly upwind, to fish the flies or single fly round in an arc both work on occasions.

Just as with all salmon flyfishing, fresh-run fish are the key, and one must know if the water to be fished is best in April and May or July and August. One can learn something about a length of strange river in a few days, and fish it successfully alone, but in the vastness of a loch, the knowledge of a gillie is essential.

PART THREE
Grayling

Chapter Ten

Physical and behavioural characteristics

The grayling bridges the gap between the true so-called game fish – salmon, seatrout and trout – and the coarse fish. It has the fleshy adipose fin between tail and dorsal fin that makes it a member of the aristocrats that all bear this fleshy appendage, but unlike them, it spawns in the March to May period, with the coarse fish.

The grayling is a very beautiful fish, steely-blue on the back merging into silvery-white flanks tinged with startling lengthways lines of dark blue-grey. The vast, sail-like dorsal fin is greenish-blue with beautiful markings that vary in hue from dark reddish brown to coral. Overall, the grayling is tinged with shades of lilac and the sides are spotted in a random fashion with black.

Its underslung, diminutive mouth rather lets it down, however, for it is designed for feeding from the bottom of the river. Yet the grayling sips dry flies from the surface just as well as a trout, though it does so in a rather different way, since it has to take the fly with its body almost vertical in the water, due to that underslung mouth. And because its angle of approach to the surface has to be so steep, it tends to misjudge its interception, and misses more flies than does the trout.

Location

Grayling cannot tolerate water that is warm or polluted; it is far more susceptible in both these respects than the trout or the salmon. Cool, clean, fast-flowing water is what the grayling has to have, and if those conditions change, the grayling tends to migrate upstream, where the water is likely to be more pure. Many of today's rivers that held grayling almost from source to mouth a few years ago, now have them only in their headwaters.

Yet the range of the grayling is wide: in Britain it is equally at home in the Hampshire chalk-streams and in the fast, stony rivers of the North of England and in Scotland. It grows large in Scandinavian rivers, specially those in Finland, where fish of 2.2 kg (5 lb) are not exactly uncommon. Fish of 3.6 kg (8 lb) have been caught in Lapland. In the English chalk-streams, a 900 g (2 lb) fish is a good one, a 1.3 kg (3 lb) one a rarity. In the north of England, the fish are slimmer and 900 g (2 lb) is considered a big fish. Grayling are very good to eat, either split and grilled or fried, or smoked.

Grayling live on a diet of mainly freshwater shrimps and nymphs of varied

The grayling is a beautiful fish and here erects its battle flag, that vast, sail-like dorsal fin.

water-bred flies, although they like to eat worms, maggots and even the breadbaits of coarse fishermen. They are at their best in the period from September until after Christmas, and even in October and November, they may be taken on the fly, both sunken and floating, when the water is clear and the weather mild. In summer, grayling tend to be rather slimy and soft to touch, but from September on they become firm and strong, no doubt because the cooling water is more to their liking.

Trout fishermen, especially those who fish the chalk-streams, tend to dislike grayling. They are said to compete with the trout for the available food and the keepers of chalk-streams tend to make an annual cull, either by netting or by letting fishermen catch and kill them after the trout season has closed. Also, some trout fishermen do not like, when they present their fly to a sipping rise on a summer day, to bring the fish up and hook it, only to find it is a grayling and not a trout. The fact that summer grayling are not in the peak of condition until September – and so cannot fight so well – is ignored by the single-minded trout flyfisher. I would rather flyfish for grayling on a chalk-stream than I would for trout: the trout may be wild, but are more likely to have been stocked; the grayling is always a wild fish and that, plus its beauty and strong fighting qualities after September, makes it a very desirable quarry for an increasing number of fishermen rather disillusioned with hatchery-reared trout.

Grayling tend to swim in shoals of half-a-dozen to more than fifty fish. They like fairly shallow, gravel-bottomed areas where the water flows smoothly, although they will also lie in deep, eddying pools in the dead of winter. Although they are just as easily scared as trout, by a heavy footfall, or a silhouette, or shadow falling over them, they are easier to catch than trout. Fish after fish may be taken from the same shoal, provided you do not let the hooked fish splash about too much, but drag it downstream and away from its fellows. Also, grayling will rise repeatedly to a dry fly, missing it several times but then taking it firmly on, perhaps, the tenth attempt.

They can pull very hard indeed, possibly harder than a trout of comparable size, and they fight with a strange, twisting motion, rolling over and over or using that huge dorsal fin as a parachute against the pull of the line. Sometimes grayling fight wildly, leaping like trout.

Scare a shoal and they will scatter, up or down the river, but providing you kneel quietly out of sight, they are most likely to return to the spot within five minutes, and are then immediately catchable again.

Tackle

Light trout tackle, as suitable for dry fly and nymph on small rivers, is fine for grayling fishing, but err on the light side, using a double-taper size 3 or 4 floating line and a very flexible matching rod of 2.60–2.75 m ($8\frac{1}{2}$–9 ft), since the fast strikes needed to hook them are better cushioned with such a rod.

The fishing is far more enjoyable if you can see the fish in the river, and the clearer rivers, especially the crystalline chalk-streams, are best. North of England rivers often colour up with rain and make visual fishing impossible, although casting a dry fly to the rising fish is then a profitable and enjoyable technique. I prefer to fish for grayling I can see, using the sunken nymph, and only two patterns are necessary: a size 12 or 14 Pheasant Tail Nymph and the late Frank Sawyer's Grayling Bug, which is simply a size 12 or 14 hook with a leaded shank over which is wrapped a spindle-shaped body of fawn-grey wool that becomes an olive hue when wet. Another name for this excellent shrimp-imitating pattern is the Killer Bug.

Provided the water remains clear, which is often the case on the chalk-streams, grayling may be spotted in the river even in the dead of winter, and they may still be caught on a leaded, deeply-sunk nymph. For those trout fishermen who like to keep their flyrods in action when the trout season is but a memory and when the new season is many months away, the grayling is a gift of the gods.

In the past few years, the grayling's place in flyfishing has become elevated and the keepers of trout streams will often permit you to fish for grayling after September for a small fee, instead of netting the fish and dumping them on the bank. An indication of this new interest in grayling was the formation in 1978 of The Grayling Society in Britain, which aims to popularize the fish and seek more knowledge of its natural history and ways.

Chapter Eleven

Dry fly and nymph fishing for grayling

Dry fly fishing

There are special dry flies for grayling, most of them rather fat-bodied affairs with just a hackle, no wing and, often, a short tail of silk of feather fibre, red or yellow. They have names like Red Tag, Treacle Parkin, Green Insect, and various Bumbles. But grayling are not fastidious. They will take almost any small trout fly, and sizes 14 and 16 are generally the most acceptable.

Some fishermen claim to be able to differentiate between a trout rise and a grayling rise to a fly, but it is very tricky. Certainly grayling tend to make very tiny, sipping rises when small flies, land-bred or water-bred, are about, but then so can a trout. Both trout and grayling sometimes rise in fast water to a floating fly with gay abandon, sending spray flying in their eagerness to grab the morsel.

When trout are set on taking hatched flies, however, they tend to station themselves near the surface of the river, from where they can judge their interception of current-borne food more easily; grayling tend to lie much deeper and this, coupled with that small underslung mouth, makes the interception quite a feat, so they often miss. But when they do take, they snap up the fly at speed, and flick down again. Trout, by comparison, take in a leisurely manner.

Thus, when fishing the dry fly to grayling, it pays to be on the *qui vive* for the rise. As soon as the fish breaks the surface, tighten quickly. One cannot be too quick to sink the barb in a grayling.

The best of all dry fly fishing for grayling comes in September and throughout the warm days of October, when there are still good numbers of various flies to attract them to surface-feed, and shallow, swift water only 60 cm (2 ft) deep over gravel produces excellent sport. The fish can be located with polarizing glasses and, with careful fishing, fish after fish may be taken. With the characteristically small flies that the grayling prefer, a thin leader tippet – about 900 g (2 lb) test – is called for, and I have known fish accept a fly gleefully on that but turn away from the same pattern on a 1.3 kg (3 lb) tippet.

Unlike trout, however, grayling are not put off by a dry fly that creates a certain amount of drag; indeed, some drag is very often more attractive to the grayling than a fly floating down perfectly drag-free. I have often cast my fly almost square to the current, or even a little downstream and across, and

A fly-caught grayling
comes to net –

directly the fly begins to drag a grayling will detach itself from the shoal and come up to grab it.

Although grayling are never as fussy about the exact copy of the fly that is hatching most profusely, and which they are mainly feeding on, as are trout, they can sometimes be quite selective. This selective feeding occurs more when there are heavy hatches of Pale Watery Olives or, in October more than in September, Large Dark Olives.

Also unlike trout, grayling will shoal in open, shallow reaches of the river where there is little cover in the form of weeds or overhanging foliage. Their camouflage, though, is often excellent, and it can take time to locate them. The fish in one shoal are usually all about the same size, and if your first casts produce fish of around 450 g (8 oz), it is unlikely, but not impossible, that you will catch bigger fish in that place.

and it's a very big one.

Grayling may be caught by wet fly fishing downstream and across, casting to cover the river at random and working downstream, but just as with all fish that take the fly fished downstream, many fish will be hooked momentarily and then shake free. The angle of pull is all wrong. But many fish are caught each year in this way, and small spider-type flies work well.

Nymph fishing

Nymph fishing is the best sport of all with grayling. The water may be only 60 cm (2 ft) deep, or less, or up to 1.2 m (4 ft) or more, but provided the fish have been located, great bags may be taken.

Either the Pheasant Tail Nymph or Sawyer's Killer Bug could be successful, with plenty of lead under the dressings for water 1.2 m (4 ft) deep or more, and for water that is less than that depth but flowing briskly. It is a real problem to get the nymph down to the fish lying on the bottom, and they seem to like it when it is actually trundling along the gravel.

I like best to be able to watch the fish take the nymph, rather than fish by watching the leader for signals of takes. Kneeling to take advantage of background cover, and casting upstream or up and across, with a 3.6 m (12 ft) leader to enable me to drop the nymph well above the shoal leaders without showing them the line, and thus permit the nymph time to sink before it drifts down to them, I have passed many a pleasant autumn day catching maybe thirty fish in two or three hours. If you can conceal rod and arm movements, perhaps by using the rod almost parallel with the water, long casting is not necessary. Indeed, it is a serious disadvantage, because it does not permit you to see the fish that darts from the shoal and turns sideways to snap at your offering, and it also makes for a slower reaction, due to the delay in the tightening action with a long line on the water.

Dexterity in recovering slack line as the line floats back with the current must be competent if the lifting of the rod to hook the taking fish is to be done quickly. Figure-eighting is all right for the slower water, but for fast runs it cannot keep up, and a stripping technique is called for.

Perhaps due to that underslung little mouth, grayling are more difficult to hook than trout, ignoring the problems of fishing depth or the height they must rise, at times, to a dry fly, and many fish will come unstuck, whichever way you choose to fish. However, on the credit side, the mouth of a grayling is quite tough and rubbery inside the lips, and a hook penetrating that area seldom comes out.

Grayling should be played gently in fast water, for they can pull very hard indeed, and they can either bend or break the tiny hooks used. I have taken few grayling much over 900 g (2 lb), and most grayling fishermen who use the fly will admit to a similar history, if they are truthful, but I did once lose an enormous specimen, estimated at 1.8 kg (4 lb), on the Test a few years ago. And it was my own fault.

I hooked it on a size 12 Killer Bug and it led me a merry dance all over the river for ten minutes, boring deeply and making 18.3 m (20 yd) runs. It was not until I unclipped the net that I first realized just how big that fish was, and I tried to bring it the last metre or so upstream to the net, instead of trying to get below it. Of course, the hook broke in the bend when the fish was 15 cm (6 in) from the rim of the net. I doubt I will ever see his like again.

PART FOUR

Coarse fish on the fly

Chapter Twelve

Chub, dace and rudd

Nintey-nine per cent of coarse fish are taken on bait, either float-fishing in one way or another, or legering. But much of the food of the coarse fish is the same as that taken by trout and grayling, including shrimps, nymphs, winged flies and little fish, and flyfishing can take many fish, especially on warm summer days when bait fishing is often relatively ineffective.

Chub

From the opening of the coarse fishing season on 16 June until well into October, chub and dace in the rivers are often feeding well on surface flies, and quite often flies may be fished in very weedy, shallow areas where it is difficult to fish a bait. A chub of 1.3 kg (3 lb) or more, hooked on light trout tackle, can be a real handful, especially on its first rush for cover. They can be found rising regularly under bankside foliage, under steep banks, or in narrow channels between the streamer-weeds.

Normal trout fishing tactics will work well, but should the fish not be very forthcoming, there is a useful method of attack that can prove invaluable. It involves dropping the fly not above the fish, in the normal way, but just downstream of its position or its last rise. Very often, a chub will turn round to follow the fly downstream for a metre, then suck it in with a loud slurp.

Traditionally, chub flies are rather large, fuzzy creations, dressed Palmer-style on size 10 and 12 hooks, but they will take most of the trout dry flies, a Coachman, Grey Duster, Black Palmer or Zulu being established favourites.

In seatrout and salmon rivers containing chub, they are often taken on flies fished for those two species, and I have taken some extra-large chub using reservoir trout lures 5 cm (2 in) or more long, fished down and across on a slow-sinking or sink-tip line. I imagine that these big, streamer-type flies are taken for small fish, since chub are very fond of minnows and small fry of other fish.

Dace

A shoal of dace delicately dimpling the surface of a smooth, shallow, gravelly glide, taking tiny insects, can be a real challenge to any dry fly man. A 680 or 900 g ($1\frac{1}{2}$ or 2 lb) tippet and size 16 and even 18 flies may be called for, and because dace are shoal fish, and easily scared, a careful presentation is necessary to fool more than the odd fish. Dace also rise much more quickly than trout –

Flyfishing for coarse fish
on a Midlands brook.

and maybe faster than grayling – but in spite of their speed of the rise, the fish may only make a tiny dimple as your fly disappears.

Dace rarely exceed 225 g ($\frac{1}{2}$ lb), but they can be very good fun on light gear, and they will often continue to rise throughout the bright light and heat of a hot summer day.

Rudd

Rudd are fish of lakes, canals and sluggish rivers. They are a beautiful bronze and gold with deep flanks, upturned mouths (ideal for surface feeding, unlike the grayling's) and fins that vary from rich red to bright orange. In some lakes and pools they can reach 900 g (2 lb) quite regularly and they fight well, too.

They take nymphs and dry flies readily and fishing from the bank, or from a boat anchored near the edges of weed-beds where they love to cruise, can produce excellent results.

Rudd are one of the few fish taken on fly that can be lured to the surface by groundbaiting. Some flyfishermen may not like the idea of resorting to the coarse fishermen's technique of luring fish by feeding them, but a big shoal of rudd can be kept within casting range by throwing out a few crusts of dry bread. If the floating bread drifts away on the wind, it may be tied to thin cord with a stone at the other end, and anchored in position. Rudd love to take floating bread on the surface, and while doing so they are just as happy to take a dry fly.

Other coarse fish

In recent years, there has been a little more interest in flyfishing for coarse fish and among the other species that are basically non-predatory (on other fish) which have been taken are roach, tench and carp. I have taken quite a few roach, including some good fish over 445 g (1 lb), on dry fly, and a few tench on sunken nymphs, fishing still-water trout style. And although I have never caught a carp on fly, not having fished for them in this way, I do know of fishermen who have done so. They tell me that a white fly, to imitate an evening-flying moth, and fished over the surface like a sedge is fished for trout, is quite effective. Carp have also taken deep-fished nymphs, and fish of well over 9 kg (20 lb) have been taken in this way by American flyfishers, who are a little more adventurous than their British counterparts.

As a final thought, I once had a very hard take on a size 8 Teal, Blue and Silver while fishing for seatrout in a weir-pool at 11.30 at night on the Eastern Rother in Sussex. I tightened and felt a thumping sensation as a fish moved off in a dour run. I was very surprised indeed a few minutes later when I slid a 1.1 kg (2½ lb) bream over the rim of my landing net.

There is certainly a great deal of scope for flyfishing for species of coarse fish not regularly sought in this way. In continental Europe, barbel are taken on big, leaded nymphs, which is more food for thought.

Since most coarse fish are returned alive to the water, because they are not considered worth eating and for reasons of conservation, the fly is a good method, since nearly every fish is hooked lightly in the mouth and is little damaged before being slipped back to fight again.

Chapter Thirteen

Pike and perch

In comparison with most other coarse fish species – including those mentioned in the previous chapter – pike and perch are considered predators because they feed only on animals whereas chub, dace, rudd, and so on, eat animals in the form of insects, molluscs and crustaceans as well as vegetable matter: weeds, seeds and fruits, for example. Only the chub, among those listed, also eats other fish regularly.

What is not generally appreciated, however, is that while pike subsist largely on a diet of small fish, they also eat a lot of small animals, including shrimps, worms (when available), large nymphs (specially those of damsel and dragonflies) and very large quantities of midge pupae and larvae where these are literally carpeting the bottom of still waters and slow-moving rivers and drainage channels. Examination of the stomach contents of large numbers of small pike, fish of about 1.3 kg (3 lb) to 3.6 kg (8 lb), has revealed this mode of feeding to me, and there have been odd specimens that have contained nothing else but insects. One fish of about 1.8 kg (4 lb) caught by a friend on a trout lure contained only midge pupae – enough to make two double handfuls!

In most environments, perch eat more insects than they do small fish, although they will take advantage of large concentrations of tiddlers, when they occur, such as spawning minnows and sticklebacks.

And since these facts illustrate that the diet of perch, and many small pike, is very similar to that of trout, it is not very surprising that trout flyfishing tactics used on still waters, both to imitate small fish and subsurface insect life, will catch both pike and perch extremely successfully.

Pike

To take the pike first, it must be admitted that, in spite of its propensity in some waters containing rich larders of bottom-dwelling insects to feed heavily on them, the fish is primarily a fish-eater. That means that lures from about 3.2 cm ($1\frac{1}{4}$ in) in length up to around 7.5 cm (3 in), which simulate small fish, are very useful pike flies. They should be fished to imitate small fish, and this does not mean that they have to be stripped at speed through the water – rather the opposite.

In reservoirs and lakes containing trout and pike, most fishermen using lures will occasionally hook a pike by accident while after trout. Sometimes, if the hook is lodged near the front of the mouth, out of the way of the fish's sharply pointed teeth, the pike will be landed. Often, though, the fish takes the fly well back into its mouth and the fairly thin leaders used for trout are easily severed by being rubbed over the teeth during the fight.

Thus, some form of bite-proof section near the fly is necessary when deliberately flyfishing for pike; otherwise, normal still-water trout gear is very adequate as it stands. Provided the rod can handle line sizes 6–8, it will do the job well.

Having caught a fair number of pike by accident on lures, I decided several years ago to set out deliberately to catch pike. The decision was taken in the dead of winter at a period when I was becoming bored and wanted to feel a flyrod in my hand again, and get a line moving nicely through the air. I used a 2.75 cm (9 ft) rod, a double-taper slow-sinking line and a lure with a hair wing of black, blue and orange/yellow on, I think, a long-shank size 6 hook.

The water I selected for my midwinter exercise was a slow-moving marsh-land dyke on the Kent marshlands in the Rother Valley, and on the day it was quite turgid, although the fly could be seen about 30 cm (1 ft) or so down. To cut a long story short, I caught seven pike in about two and a half hours during my session, but none at all until I slowed down my initial fast retrieve to a very slow one, using long, smooth pulls.

Since then, I have taken fair numbers of pike on the fly, none exceeding about 3.6 kg (8 lb), although I know specimens over 9 kg (20 lb) have been taken by other flyfishers. What has come out of my personal experiences has been that pike in rivers with any reasonable flow do not usually take the fly very well. The best locations for the technique are still waters or very slow-flowing rivers, canals or marshland drains. And if the water is reasonably shallow, say up to about 2.4 m (8 ft), then so much the better. I have no doubt that fishing 6 m (20 ft) down with a very heavy, fast-sinking line and a lure from 7.5–10 cm (3–4 in) long will take pike – and perhaps better ones than I feel the need to engage.

On moderately light still-water trout tackle, even a pike of 1.8 kg (4 lb) is good fun. They fight, usually, in a very lively manner and jump more frequently than when hooked on a spinner, plug or live and dead fish baits.

The leader for pike can be about 2.75 m (9 ft) long, made from a level length of 3.6–4.5 kg (8–10 lb) test nylon with about 15 cm (6 in) or so of 6.8 kg (15 lb) nylon joined to the end which takes the fly. This is usually sufficiently robust to prevent a pike's teeth cutting through. A safe way of attaching this heavy 'collar' to the main part of the leader involves applying a flame carefully to one end of the 6.8 kg (15 lb) nylon until it melts and forms a globule. Let this harden again and then form a nail/needle knot around the nylon behind it with the main leader material. Pull the knot up tight and slide it forward to jam behind the swelled end of the collar. A touch of cyanoacrylate adhesive will help make the junction even more secure.

Most of my deliberate flyfishing for pike has been done in autumn and winter, and a sinking line, to fish the fly slowly about 30 cm (1 ft) above the bottom, seems to be the most killing method. However, in summertime, when pike may often be located as they lie just below the surface among weedbeds, sunken logs and over submerged lily-pads, I have taken them by casting a lure on a floating or sink-tip line to a point ahead and beyond them – without letting them see the line – and fishing the fly back quite quickly, in 30 cm (1 ft) strips, to suggest a tiny fish, alarmed and seeking to get away. It seems to arouse the pike's predatory instinct immediately. At all other times, however, the sunk line and slow-moving lure has done better.

When the lure is being trickled back slowly just above the bottom, the takes of pike can be surprisingly gentle: just a slow, shuddering stoppage of the fly's progress, at which time a firm pull usually sinks the hook. Pike are rarely missed on the slow fly. Perhaps, on reflection, some of the fish take the lure for a large, bottom-dwelling insect, as well as, at other times, a small fish. Pike are lazy fish in cold water and like to lie in ambush, in a depression in the bottom or along undercut or steep banks, from where they can make a quick, short dart to secure their prey, rather than engage in a long chase. Pike are not equipped for long, fast chases; their propelling fins – tail, dorsal and anal – are all grouped well together for a quick, sharp burst of speed from a standing start.

When taking the slow lure, they must just sidle up and open their mouths, then close them again. That would bring about the effect I have outlined.

The pike fly I evolved for my own fishing, which was named the Esox-it, for no other reason than that *Esox lucius* is the pike's scientific name and because when the fly passes the fish, 'he socks it', has proved very successful and the dressing is given, with other recommended flies, in chapter 15. Many other lures of the streamer and bucktail type will catch pike and among the best are those with mobile wings of marabou – the fluffy feathers from the upper parts of the legs of turkeys.

A landing net with a frame about 60 cm (2 ft) across and with a bag net at least that deep will accommodate pike up to 4.5 kg (10 lb) with ease, but if you expect to catch pike bigger than that frequently, then a small gaff may be better. Pike are not gaffed in the body like salmon – or should not be – since most of them are returned to the water alive. Instead, the small but strong gaff hook is inserted only just inside the bowed front jawbone in the lower jaw, preferably from underneath, and the fish *slid* up the bank or over the gunwale of a boat. The fish should not be lifted, unless it is to be killed for the table, because its weight may tear the jaw and result in death if it is put back.

Although pike have big, pointed teeth and their jaw-closing power is considerable, there is no need to be afraid of unhooking the fish for this reason. A thick leather glove may be used to hold the lower jaw down while the fly is removed, or a short piece of softwood, about 5 cm (2 in) in thickness, can be placed across the open mouth to act as a gag while the job is done.

Pike are, by the way, very good to eat and very popular in France and Germany, although seldom used in Britain. Fish up to about 3.6 kg (8 lb) make the best eating, and they may be baked or fried in cutlets, suitably seasoned. My favourite recipe involves simmering the pike in salted water, afterwards flaking and deboning the cold flesh, mixing it with mashed potato and seasoning into fishcakes. Fried golden-brown and crisp, they are delicious.

Hen pike grow much bigger than cock fish. Any pike over 4.5 kg (10 lb) is almost certainly a hen and the largest male pike I have ever heard of weighed 6.3 kg (14 lb).

Perch

Perch, too, are best sought with the fly in still water or water that is very slow flowing. In lakes and reservoirs where perch share the water with trout, they are frequently taken, especially during periods of hot, settled sunny weather, when trouting with a deeply sunk nymph or with flashy traditional wet flies such as the Butcher, Alexandra, Teal and Red. They will also follow and snap up a smallish lure, up to about 5 cm (2 in) long.

Little needs to be said about catching perch on the fly; the usual trouting techniques work well; but a fly with a little red in its dressing seems to work better than most, and one keeper on a reservoir I know used to like to fish for perch better than for the trout, and he used a fly with a bright scarlet wool body, ribbed with silver tinsel and with a mallard wing. He said he caught as many perch – sometimes fifty in a half-day session – when the wing had been torn off by the capture of so many fish! Sizes 8 or 10 were his favourites.

On hot, bright days in summer, a slow-sinking weight-forward or shooting-taper line fished 90 cm (1 yd) off the bottom in 3 m (10 ft) or more of water works well. Small, deep bays, especially if they abound with sunken trees and other snags, are the favoured perch habitat, and the water off the faces of stone-built reservoir dams can often be very productive.

Perch are essentially shoaling fish, at least until they reach weights much over 900 g (2 lb), and once a good shoal has been located, and providing it does not decide to move off, it should be possible to catch several fish from that shoal. A shoal can contain hundreds of fish and their weights may vary from less than 225 g ($\frac{1}{2}$ lb) up to well over 900 g (2 lb).

Perch from clean water are delicious to eat – many prefer them to trout, as did my reservoir keeper. They provide excellent sport at times when trout can be difficult to catch, providing a useful stop-gap between the morning rise and evening rise on a hot sunny day. They do not fight very hard, as a rule, but their green, black and vermillion colouration, and their value as food, adequately makes up for those shortcomings.

PART FIVE

The do-it-yourself flyfisher

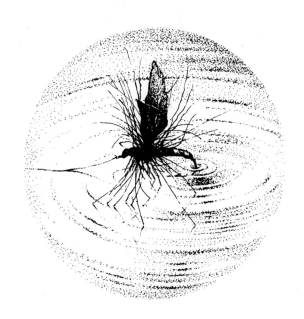

Chapter Fourteen

Tackle

I have an abiding passion for really good fishing tackle. I cannot fish well with a shoddy rod or one with chips in its varnish or its whippings frayed. When reels become worn with use, their enamel scratched and grazed, I cannot rest until I have stripped off the paintwork and then polished the alloy until it shines like silver. Even worse, for me, are rods that have poor actions due to faulty basic design, or rods made up with excessively heavy metalwork on them.

Customizing rods

Any rods I have bought, or been given, ready made, I have usually stripped down and rewhipped and varnished within a very short time, making minor alterations to handle length and thickness, ring types and positions, producing a far more classy rod as a result; and, more important, one that fits my styles of casting and fishing. In spite of being 80 kg and 1.8 m (12½ st and 6 ft), I have hands in which a 2.5 cm (1 in) thick cork handle feels like an axe-handle. They are small and stubby-fingered, and unless my rod handles are slim, I cannot grip them delicately and fish the same way. Put it like this: could you write neatly with a 2.5 cm (1 in) thick pencil?

There are many advantages to being able to make and alter tackle, not least one of saving money. It's not really a saving, because the money actually saved on tackle can be spent on access to better fishing than otherwise I would be able to afford. There is little sense in fishing mediocre waters with expensive, shop-bought tackle.

I have already touched on the simplicity of building a flyrod from modern blanks of graphite, glass-fibre and split bamboo cane in chapter 3, but a little expansion, to encourage those who still believe rodmaking is beyond them, is appropriate.

Some companies supply complete rod kits, with everything in them, including varnish and thread and suggested ring positions, and many of these are very good value. However, unless there are alternative rings, handle lengths, shapes and thicknesses from which to choose, which again increases the price, it is better to buy the blank and the other bits and pieces separately.

Many kits are supplied with the cork handles, ready shaped, glued on and fitted with reel seats, the ferrules or spigots fitted, and it remains only for the rings to be whipped on and the rod to be varnished several times. Such a kit can be easily completed in a long evening – say, three hours or so – although coats of varnish take at least forty-eight hours to dry properly. It is best to apply the first two coats only to the ring whippings, rubbing the varnish in well, over a period of about four days, and to apply subsequent coats to both whippings and rod surface over a period of several weeks, allowing a week between coats for hardening up. Any blemishes may then be smoothed with very fine abrasive paper, used wet, before the next coat is applied.

Some kits come with the cork handles separate – that is, the cork rings which make up the handle glued together and pre-shaped. All one has to do is slide the handle down the rod blank from the thinner end and glue the cork into place. Sometimes, however, the pre-shaped handle will be a little loose, or tight. In the former case, build up over the rod surface with a cross-wound layer of thread wound over wet glue, to tighten the fit. If the handle is too tight, it may be possible to widen it by stretching over a metal rod, or by careful work with a round file or strip of sandpaper rolled tightly into a tube.

The very best cork handles are made by gluing on cork rings, rings that are very tightly fitted on your blank, to form the handle, applying adhesive to both blank and the faces of each cork as it is forced on. Buy the best cork rings you can get, making sure they are hard, not spongy with many holes in them. The corks may be shaped to your personal whims with various grades of abrasive paper and rolling the handle on a flat surface as it is worked, to keep it round in section. Always go over to a very fine grade of abrasive before you think it is necessary, since there is no other way to obtain a really smooth, unpitted cork surface. Any small holes may be filled with a mixture of cork dust and glue, made up like plastic wood. Leave for twelve hours, at least after filling, before finally smoothing down.

Never make any handle, on a single-handed or double-handed rod, any longer than is absolutely necessary for a comfortable grip. A constant gripping position helps develop a good casting technique and retain it.

Flyrod handle shapes
1–4 Single-handed rods (trout, seatrout, salmon).
5–7 Double-handed salmon rods.

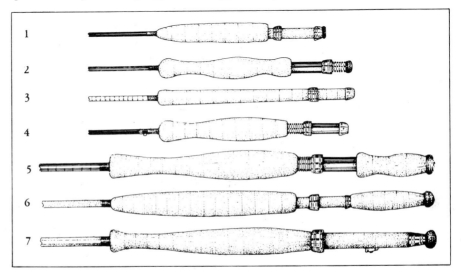

Not only that, but every unnecessary extra item you put on the rod adds to its finished weight, and on modern rods even 15 g ($\frac{1}{2}$ oz) matters. I have never felt the need for metal-screw reel fittings, even on salmon rods: they add weight and hold a reel no more firmly than does a well-fitted plain fixed metal clip and sliding ring. Also, screw reel fittings can become clogged with dirt and prove almost impossible to unfasten, no matter how careful you are.

Spacing the rings on a rod is quite an art and it is very important. The aim should be to have the line follow exactly, in a parallel fashion, the curve of the rod when it is bent into a quarter-circle, which is its optimum fighting curve. Usually, the number of rings on a rod equates to its length and one for each foot of rod is generally correct. However, the stiffness or flexibility of a rod has a bearing on the number of rings fitted, and where; and on very light rods – for use with size 3–4 lines – the rings should be the lightest obtainable and the minimum number compatible with a reasonable curve of rod and line.

Heavy rings and too many rings can ruin the casting action of a very light rod blank – so always use light snake rings on such rods, never Fuji rings or bridge type. Remember: everything you put on a rod has to be cast by that rod in addition to the weight of line it is made to cast. It is easy to overload a good light blank, and many factories do this without realizing their error.

Rods with tip actions – that is, with most of the bending taking place near the tip and down to some 75 cm (2$\frac{1}{2}$ ft) from the hand – need few rings in the lower section, since it bends little, but plenty near the tip, where the bend can be acute. Similarly, rods which bend almost into the cork handles need rings spaced fairly evenly throughout, rather than rapidly decreasing in spacing towards the tip, as is required by the tip-action or fast-action rod.

Always whip rings on tightly with the finest thread you can work with, of nylon or Terylene. Both are rot-proof. Most factory-made rods are whipped by women and they do not have the necessary strength to apply sufficient constant tension to the thread, the result being that rings can become loose on the rod after very little use.

Most graphite and hollow-glass blanks are now supplied with the spigot joints ready fitted. Some cane rod kits have the metal ferrules fitted, too. Either are quite easy to fit at home anyway. Spigots are tapered and are simply dropped down the tube from the larger end until they emerge from the narrow end. Prior to doing so, smear a little Araldite for the last 5 cm (2 in) or so of the narrow end, inside the blank, of course. And when the spigot emerges, turn it round, so as to spread the adhesive evenly. Make sure sufficient spigot protrudes to make a good joint with the next section of the rod before setting it aside to dry. If the spigot jams on the wet adhesive, push it through with a thin stick, kept by for that purpose. It is best to protect the end of the blank against splitting while the spigot is being pushed out, with a rough, tight whipping or a layer of tightly-wound adhesive tape. The mated joint should have a 6 mm ($\frac{1}{4}$ in) gap between the sections.

A whipping at least 2.5 cm (1 in) long should be made tightly over the female part of any spigot joint, and another about 12 mm ($\frac{1}{2}$ in) long over the end of the blank into which the spigot has been stuck.

For cane rods – of which there are comparatively few in use today – splint-end ferrules of nickel silver or bronzed brass are usual, the former being preferable. The splint ends are to prevent a sudden sharp change in stiffness in the junction of cane and metal, against which the cane may shear, and the six splints should be filed to a feather edge and fitted to cover the six flats of the cane. The cane may need to be rounded slightly where it fits into the ferrule and the splints lightly tapped into place over the flats with a small hammer, then being roughly lashed down over a glue-film.

When dry, the splints are whipped firmly with thread, to match the whippings used for the rings, or in a contrasting colour. When whipping a rod, always hold the spool of thread in the palm of one hand and turn the rod away from that hand with the other hand, guiding the turns of thread tightly, each butting up to the next. Keep the tension constant. When beginning a whipping, by the way, it pays to moisten the end you lay on the rod with saliva, to hold it in position, while the first turns over it are made.

Second-hand flyrods are often very good buys, and provided the actual blank itself is straight and sound, and the joints fit well, or may be tightened up easily or replaced, pay no attention to a rough, chipped varnish surface or rusty rings and frayed whippings. The rod can be stripped down to the bare graphite, glass or cane and made to look like new again – or even better.

Cut the whippings over the ring feet with a scalpel or new razor-blade, which prevents cutting into the blank, and unroll the thread. Coat with paint stripper – 60 cm (2 ft) at a time – and when the varnish has bubbled, strip off lengthways with a sharp knife held with its blade at a right angle to the surface. Wash off the residual stripper with water or white spirit, according to the maker's instructions. I have never found any material to be adversely affected by stripper if it is used in this way.

When the whole rod has been stripped, examine the joints and make any adjustments or replacements before proceeding further. Loose spigots may be tightened up by first wrapping the female part with Scotch tape and cutting off maybe 6 mm ($\frac{1}{4}$ in) of the blank with a fine hacksaw – cutting through the tape prevents the blank splitting.

Loose metal ferrules can often be tightened up by gently tapping the female with a wooden mallet with the ferrule on a block of hardwood, turning the ferrule as you tap. This must be done with care, with frequent testing for size.

When the rod is ready to be re-ringed and whipped, smooth its surface with very fine silicon-carbide paper (such as grade P600A of English Abrasives) used dry on cane but wet on glass and graphite.

Flydressing

Without dressing your own flies, the sport will always be lacking something. Quite apart from the undoubted long-term saving made on flies, there is great pleasure and fascination in dressing flies for all kinds of fishing, be they imitative nymphs and dry flies for trout and grayling or big, garish tubes for spring salmon.

One soon becomes a veritable magpie, picking up dead birds, squirrels and rabbits on the roadsides, and moulted feathers from various birds at the waterside. Spiriting away bits of coloured wool and silks from the wife's workbasket becomes an art! The labrador's tail is not sacrosanct to the true *aficionado*, who also may be seen skulking at jumble sales to buy old fur stoles, feather boas, hats and the like.

The essentials for flydressing are not too expensive. The basic needs are a good, lever-operated vice (I recommend the Sunrise Super AA as the best value); at least two bobbin-holders for your tying thread; two pairs of hackle pliers (for winding hackles and other materials); two pairs of scissors, one small and finely pointed for delicate cutting of silks and feathers, the other larger, for heavier cutting work; a dubbing needle with a half-hitch tool at the end of the handle; an eye surgeon's scalpel and a supply of blades; a bobbin-threader; and a very fine, pointed paintbrush. A pair of tweezers, for picking up small hooks and other items, are also helpful.

Not essential, but a boon on long sessions at the vice, is an anglepoise lamp with a steady, heavy base.

As I have already said, many of the necessary materials may be picked up on the roads, in the countryside or purloined from various sources. In addition, if you are a shooter, the plumage of pheasants, especially the centre tails of old cock birds, partridges, ducks and so-called vermin – magpies, crows, rooks and jays – will take on a new importance. So will the tails of grey squirrels, the skins of rabbits, hares, moles and foxes, all of which provide hair and/or fur for various uses in flydressing. The body and longer tail hairs of English fallow deer are very good for Muddler Minnows and as salmon fly wings and lure wings respectively, and the body hair of roe deer is also good for Muddlers. If you do not shoot or have no friends who do, then make friends with your local game dealer or poultry butcher.

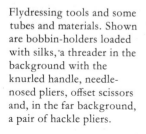

Flydressing tools and some tubes and materials. Shown are bobbin-holders loaded with silks, a threader in the background with the knurled handle, needle-nosed pliers, offset scissors and, in the far background, a pair of hackle pliers.

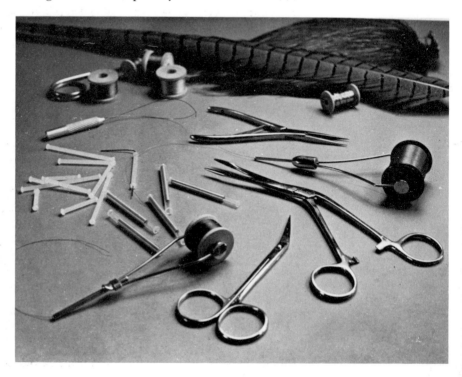

Never, ever refuse anything anybody offers you for your flydressing materials collection. Always be thankful, even if you put it in the dustbin or burn it five minutes later. Refusal of a stinking dead squirrel may lose you a recently-killed whole fox in the future. Once people get to know that you value such victims of modern traffic, they will keep a look-out for you. Many birds are protected from deliberate killing but fall victim to cars, particularly early in the morning; these include blackbirds, moorhens, coots, and so on. A find to be celebrated is that of a dead swan or wild goose or heron. From their wing and shoulder feathers come some of the finest herls for fly bodies, and the white feathers are easily dyed.

But many other items need to be bought from the various firms dealing in flydressing materials: such things as cock hackle capes, in various colours, for dry flies and salmon flies and the wings of trout lures and streamers; hen capes for wet flies and nymphs; tying threads; body silk flosses in various hues; flat, oval and wire tinsels for ribbing bodies; and some of the other body materials unobtainable from free sources – seal fur in various colours, polypropylene fibre, ostrich and peacock herls, among others.

Take this advice: never buy any body floss other than Pearsall's Marabou, which is pure silk. Body floss made from man-made fibres and from Indian sources is useless for producing good, translucent fly bodies. The best nylon tying threads come from Danville's, an American company, but with many outlets in the United Kingdom and elsewhere.

Flydressing is a very large subject and recommended books on the subject are included in the list at the end of this chapter. There are just one or two suggestions that I would like to give that might make a useful contribution to both experienced and tyro flydressers. I do not pretend they are brand-new ideas but they are certainly not put into use as often as they deserve to be.

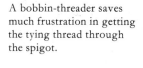

A bobbin-threader saves much frustration in getting the tying thread through the spigot.

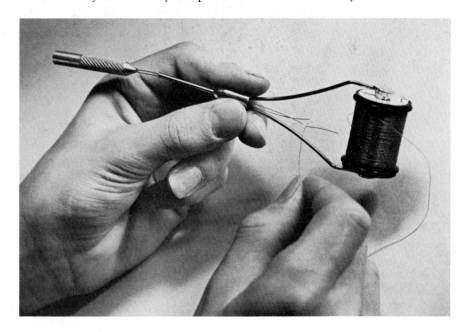

When making a body completely covered with flat tinsel, always tie it in at the eye end of the shank, wind it down to the bend over a layer of tying thread that has been anointed with clear head varnish, and then coat the first layer with varnish before finishing the body with a second, butting layer up to where the body was first tied in. Such bodies will not come unravelled in hard use.

Similarly, when winding bodies of herls, wind them – from bend towards the eye this time – over a layer of thread coated with clear head varnish while the varnish is still tacky. This sticks the herls down firmly, whereas without this treatment, herl bodies are usually destroyed by the teeth of the first fish caught.

I have already mentioned, earlier in these pages, that excellent transmitted-light effects can be obtained by winding herls and dubbed translucent fur bodies over an underbody of silver tinsel or Lurex. I stress it again, and add that most insect bodies, and those of other items of trout food, are not made up of one solid colour but are more usually a combination of several colours or shades which give an over-all effect. Therefore, experiment when dressing your imitative fly bodies and try mixtures of various colours to produce natural effects. Some of the Irish flydressers, including both Michael Rogan and Robert McHaffie, whose products are commercial, have been responsible for superb mixtures of colours, especially in dubbed bodies.

Do not be frightened off flydressing because you feel your fingers are too clumsy; some of the best flydressers I know have hands like hams. Neatness and dexterity comes with practice, and some of the books suggested in the special chapter will prove valuable guides, although with some aspects nothing replaces an hour or two of tuition by a competent dresser. There are many about and there is bound to be somebody within reasonable reach who will help you, either free or for a small fee. Many adult evening classes include flydressing courses.

Finally, on the subject of flydressing, the only really impossible manual situation for the work is rough, chapped hands. Rough, hard skin prevents any serious flydressing, since the gossamer threads will catch up and break to cause mind-bending frustration. But few can have hands so rough as a working farmer's, and I know several who manage, in spite of the problem. The answer is to keep the hands soft with one of the many preparations on the market today, especially those containing lanolin. A little of one of these applied half an hour before a flydressing session will save the day.

Chapter Fifteen

Fly patterns

Still-water trout patterns

Midge pupae

Black Midge Pupa: fishing period, April to September.
HOOK: Partridge Limerick down-eye, sizes 14–10, sizes 14 and 12 best April/May.
DRESSING: Wind black pre-waxed nylon thread from 3 mm ($\frac{1}{8}$ in) behind eye to a point a little round bend. There tie in narrow silver Lurex or tinsel. The abdomen is made from either black-dyed swan, goose or condor herls, wound over wet Cellire varnish, or from black-dyed wild rabbit fur thinly dubbed on the silk.

Wind herls or dubbed silk to within about 3 mm ($\frac{1}{8}$ in) of the eye, to make a slim body, then rib with six to seven turns of tinsel in opposite direction to herl or silk. Tie in 2.5 cm (1 in) of hot orange Marabou floss silk, as it comes from spool in two plies, on top of hook, long end facing towards the hook bend, then 2.5 cm (1 in) of white nylon (Orlon) baby wool, one strand, on top of the floss but with the long end extending over hook eye. Wind tying silk back to where body begins and dub on a small amount of wild rabbit fur, both bluish underfur and some of the longer guard hairs. Wind a short, rounded thorax, then bring orange floss forward over the top of the thorax and tie in firmly. Trim tag end and remove excess dubbing. Raise white wool vertically and keep it in that position as the head is formed and whip-finished. Trim off wool to within 1.5 mm ($\frac{1}{16}$ in) of eye and varnish whip-finish.

Red Midge Pupa: fishing period, late May to mid-September.
HOOK: Partridge Limerick down-eye, sizes 14–10.
DRESSING: Wind scarlet prewaxed nylon thread from 3 mm ($\frac{1}{8}$ in) behind eye to a point a little round the bend. There tie in silver Lurex or tinsel and either blood-red dyed herls – as before – or dyed wild rabbit fur dubbed on the tying thread. Wind body (herls over wet varnish) and rib quite closely with the tinsel, wound in the opposite spiral to that of the body. Eight turns are about right for a size 12 fly. Tie in white nylon baby wool tuft, as before, and then dub the thread with red-dyed wild rabbit fur and some undyed guard hairs. Wind round thorax, raise white tuft, and finish as for the black pupa.

Pale Green Midge Pupa: fishing period, mid-April to mid-September.
HOOK: Partridge Limerick down-eye, sizes 14–10.
DRESSING: Wind emerald-green thread from eye to round bend, as for previous patterns, and there tie in either gold or silver Lurex or tinsel – both are effective, gold being better on dull days. Again, the abdomen may be of very pale green-dyed swan herls, ribbed with the tinsel. The usual nylon tuft is tied in and the thorax is made by dubbing the silk with the tawny/brown fur from a wild rabbit or hare. This one, however, should have more of the long guard hairs in the dubbing.

Olive Midge Pupa: fishing period, mid-June to end of September.
HOOK: Partridge Limerick down-eye, sizes 14–10, size 14 best during evenings from July onwards.
DRESSING: Wind olive tying thread, as for other patterns, and at the same point round the hook bend, tie in silver Lurex or tinsel and swan herls dyed medium olive green. Proceed as for previous pattern from that point on.

Golden Dun Midge Pupa: fishing period, late May to mid-September.
HOOK: Partridge Limerick down-eye, size 12.
DRESSING: This pupa is dressed in exactly the same way as the olive one, but the ribbing in this case is copper coloured Lurex or tinsel and the abdomen is swan herl or turkey tail herl, dyed golden-amber. The thorax, with the usual white tuft, is this time dubbed from fawn rabbit or hare face fur with just a tiny suggestion of scarlet-dyed seal fur mixed with it.

Orange/Silver Midge Pupa: fishing period, mid-April to end of July, though this pattern may work at any time, especially during the evening.
HOOK: Partridge Limerick down-eye, sizes 10 and 12.
DRESSING: Proceed as for the Golden Dun Pupa, but use orange tying thread and reddish-orange dyed swan herls for the abdomen, ribbed very close with broad (number 14) silver Mylar – which is similar to Lurex – or tinsel of similar width. Only a narrow band of the orange herl should show between each turn of tinsel. The thorax is formed from reddish-brown dyed rabbit fur dubbed on the silk, or the ruddy herls from the centre tail feather of an old cock pheasant. The same white tuft is included.

Phantom Midge Pupa: fishing period, mid-June to mid-September.
HOOK: Partridge Limerick down-eye, sizes 16–12.
DRESSING: Wind white nylon thread from behind eye to slightly round the bend of the hook and there tie in 14 cm (6 in) of silver Lurex or Mylar so that 5 cm (2 in) extends behind the hook bend and the rest faces towards the eye. Coat thread-covered hook shank with cellulose varnish and wind tinsel that faces eye in touching turns up to the eye, again varnish first layer of tinsel, then wind back to round the hook bend. Tie in and trim surplus. Tie in two long white herls from swan shoulder feather by their tips, varnish tinsel under-body, wind tying thread up to near eye in *wide open* turns, followed by herls. Tie off herls about 3 mm ($\frac{1}{8}$ in) from eye. Rib body with tinsel left projecting

behind hook bend – about five turns for a size 14 hook. Note that this time the ribbing is wound the same way as the herls. Form very small, round thorax/head with either dark amber seal fur or buff turkey tail herls.

This pattern shines when wet and the white herl appears a very pale green, producing the translucence of the natural Phantom Pupa.

Fluorescent Red Midge Pupa: fishing period, June to September, during very late evening following red sunset.
HOOK: Partridge Limerick down-eye, size 12.
DRESSING: Wind red thread from behind eye, having tied in 10 cm (4 in) of silver Lurex or Mylar 3 mm ($\frac{1}{8}$ in) from eye, to a point a little round the bend. Tie in 7.5 cm (3 in) of black cotton (sewing) and wind red tying silk back to near eye. Varnish tying silk body and wind tinsel down to bend, re-varnish first layer of tinsel, then wind back to behind eye again. Tie off. Again varnish tinsel-covered underbody and wind black cotton in spiral up towards eye. Tie off. Tie in at same point near the eye about 10 cm (4 in) of Fire Orange Depth Ray fluorescent floss and wind it thinly to just round the bend and back up again. Tie off. Form small, ball-shaped thorax with red-dyed rabbit fur or seal fur, with the usual white wool tuft.

When wet, this fly shows a black segmented brilliant red body, with the tinsel illuminating the fluorescent floss. It will often catch trout during or after a red sunset and on into pitch darkness, when little else will take fish, but it must be fished very high in the water – not more than 7.5 cm (3 in) down.

Fluorescent Green Midge Pupa: fishing period, late May to mid-September, at dawn and especially in shallows still muddy from wind-driven wave action previous evening.
HOOK: Partridge Limerick down-eye, sizes 12 and 14.
DRESSING: Method identical to previous pattern, but substituting green tying silk and Signal Green Depth Ray fluorescent floss, and with thorax of natural rabbit (fawn) fur or hare fur, dubbed on thread, or buff turkey tail herls.

Sedge pupae

These are all dressed on long-shank hooks, preferably with forged bends, in sizes 12 and 14, or on Partridge Lure Hooks, sizes 14 and 16, which equate to the other two sizes.

Number One: fishing period mid-June to end of September, evenings best.
DRESSING: Wind pale green tying thread from 3 mm ($\frac{1}{8}$ in) behind eye to opposite the barb and there tie in fine oval gold tinsel or wire. Dub thread with amber seal fur and wind for rear two-thirds of hook. Rib in opposite spiral with tinsel or wire. Tie in on top of the hook at this point, a strip, about 3 mm ($\frac{1}{8}$ in) wide, of ruddy fibres from a cock pheasant centre tail feather, keeping them together and tying in by the tip (thin) end, the best (ruddy) side facing down towards the hook shank and the bunch angled towards the bend. Now dub the thread with pale green seal fur and wind to where the dressing

was begun. Bring pheasant fibres over back, pull taut and tie down firmly. Now tie in on each side of the thorax and angled downwards towards the hook point, two fibres from the pheasant tail, so they are about 19 mm ($\frac{3}{4}$ in) long for a size 12 hook, a little less for a size 14. Form a bold head with the tying thread, whip-finish and varnish.

Number Two: fishing period as for Number One.
DRESSING: As for Number One but substituting a 50:50 mixture of brown seal fur and wild rabbit fur for the rear part of the body and hot orange seal fur mixed in proportion of 1:4 with rabbit fur (mainly guard hairs) for front part.

Number Three: fishing period, July and August.
DRESSING: Wind brown tying thread from behind eye to opposite barb, tie in fine gold wire and dub thread with cinnamon seal fur. Wind body to where dressing was begun, rib in opposite spiral with the wire. Tie in about six of the blue fibres from a jay wing by their butts, points facing the hook point, under the hook; and on either side of the hook, and pointing down towards the point, tie in two long, speckled fibres from a guinea-fowl neck feather. Whip-finish and varnish. This pupa is dressed only on size 14 hooks and it has been extremely effective when fished quite fast during hatches of Cinnamon Sedges, the naturals of which have greenish bodies, though sometimes cinnamon. I believe the blue jay hackles, however, interplay with the body colour sufficiently to make fish take this particular pattern.

Sedge (caddis) larvae

I dress three variations to simulate the caddis dragging its case along the bottom and in the weeds, all on long-shank hooks sizes 14–10. They are dressed both leaded and unleaded and will work throughout the season.

Number One: Wind brown tying thread from just behind eye to a point opposite barb and there tie in fine copper or gold wire and four strands of greeny-bronze herls from a peacock tail plume, by the tips. Wind thread back up body, varnish and wind herls to form a tapered body, narrower at the bend, over the wet varnish. Stop just over 3 mm ($\frac{1}{8}$ in) from the eye. Wind ribbing wire. Tie in a short-fibred light brown or red game cock hackle by the stem and wind two turns. Tie off and then tie in a strand of golden-yellow wool or two herls from a swan wing feather dyed the same colour. Wind a small head, tie off and whip-finish and varnish.

Number Two: Wind brown tying thread from behind eye to opposite barb, where fine copper or gold wire is tied in and the thread is dubbed with a mixture of natural wild rabbit fur, mostly the long guard hairs, and some green and some rusty seal fur, in about equal proportions. Wind body, rib with wire and then tie in just behind the eye a short-fibred brown or black hen hackle. Wind two turns, tie off and whip-finish as usual.

Number Three: The procedure is exactly the same, but the body is of dubbed dyed black rabbit fur on black thread, ribbed with silver or gold wire, with a short-fibred hackle of red game or ginger, or a heavy dubbing 'hackle' of wild rabbit guard hairs, afterwards picking out some of the long fibres with a needle.

Damselfly nymphs

From mid-June to the end of August the large nymphs of damselflies are often taken by the bigger trout and they appear to be available in large numbers – and at the trout's mercy – when they are washed from their homes among the marginal weeds and grasses by waves during strong winds. Fishing in these windy conditions, one often sees these nymphs, some well over 2.5 cm (1 in) in length, wriggling and lashing helplessly as the waves drive them down the margins. Fish do take them when they migrate towards the margins to hatch, but the only times I find them in any numbers in the trout are during high winds. I therefore seldom fish them unless there is a strong wind.

Number One: Wind dark green thread from behind the eye of a size 10 or 12 long-shank forged hook to a point opposite the barb where two or three olive-dyed cock hackle points are tied in, to extend nearly 12 mm ($\frac{1}{2}$ in) behind the bend, and also 5 cm (2 in) of fine gold wire. Dub the thread with dark olive-green seal fur and wind a tapered body, rib in the opposite spiral with the wire, tie in and trim off. Tie in a 3 mm ($\frac{1}{8}$ in) wide strip of the fibres from a cock pheasant centre tail – or any darkish feather – so that the butts point towards the bend, then dub on golden-olive seal fur and wind a large thorax. Bring pheasant tail, or whatever, fibres over, pull taut and tie down near the eye. Strip a bunch of olive cock hackle fibres from a dyed feather, tie them in under the eye of the hook and arrange them so they slope backwards; splay the fibres so that some project at the sides. Whip-finish and varnish.

Number Two: The dark olive nymph is the most common but I have noticed a paler one and managed to catch one and produce an artificial that has done much damage. The sole difference is the body colour, which is a rich, golden-olive seal fur throughout.

Nymphs of upwing flies

I find there is little need for more than three patterns of these flies' nymphs in still-water fishing and in most circumstances one of them will do the job – the old faithful Pheasant Tail Nymph, with a little variation.

Pheasant Tail Nymph: fishing period, whole season.
HOOK: Partridge down-eye forged, flat round bend, sizes 12 and 14.
DRESSING: Wind brown nylon thread from behind eye to beginning of bend and there tie in fine gold wire (for size 14) or fine oval gold tinsel for size 12. Lay three ruddy fibres from an old cock pheasant's centre tail feather on top of the hook with about 6 mm ($\frac{1}{4}$ in) of the tips projecting aft and tie in firmly.

Do not cut off thick ends but add three more herls, tied in at the same place by their tips. Varnish silk underbody, after winding silk back to within about 3 mm ($\frac{1}{8}$ in) of the eye, and wind herls to form a tapered slim body. Wind wire or tinsel in opposite spiral, trim off wire/tinsel and bases of herls. Tie in a 3 mm ($\frac{1}{8}$ in) wide strip of any dark feather fibre – grey heron, grey goose, magpie tail, crow – on top of the hook so that the bases face towards the bend of the hook, then dub the thread with some blue underfur from a wild rabbit and a few of the guard hairs. Wind a slightly fatter thorax than the thickness of the front of the abdomen, bring the dark feather fibres over the top and tie them down, whip-finish and varnish.

I tie this nymph leaded and unleaded.

Pond Olive Nymph: fishing period, mid-May to mid-September.
HOOK: Partridge Limerick, as for midge pupae, or same as for Pheasant Tail Nymph, sizes 12 and 14.
DRESSING: Wind olive-green nylon tying thread from near eye to beginning of bend, tie in three fibres of dark olive-dyed goose or swan wing feather fibres as a tail, projecting 3 mm ($\frac{1}{8}$ in) behind bend, and fine gold wire. Wind, tying thread back to near eye, varnish turns and wind butt ends of herls to form slim body. Rib with the wire, in the opposite spiral. Tie in fibres of any dark feather as a wing-case, leaving butts facing hook bend, then dub on olive-dyed rabbit fur, wind short thorax, bring wing case over, tie down, whip-finish and varnish.

Claret Nymph: fishing period, May to September.
HOOK: Partridge Limerick down-eye or Partridge flat, forged round bend, sizes 12 and 14.
DRESSING: Wind claret nylon thread from behind eye to beginning of bend and tie in fine gold wire and three or four of the black-tipped orange fibres from a golden pheasant tippet so that only a length of orange and the black tips show: about 6 mm ($\frac{1}{4}$ in) long. Dub the thread with medium claret seal fur and wind a slim body. Rib in opposite spiral with the wire. Tie in ruddy brown cock pheasant centre tail fibres by the tips as a wing case, dub thread again and form fat thorax. Tie in short-fibred, claret-dyed cock hackle by butt, wind two turns only. Bring wing-case fibres over, forcing hackles to side, tie down, whip-finish and varnish.

To be honest, I do not know why the fish take this one so well and so frequently, but they often do so very well on a bright windy day, in June and July especially. The natural fly is found only on acid lakes and this pattern does not pretend to copy it, but is a kind of nymph fisherman's Mallard and Claret, and naturally carries the aura of this popular traditional wet fly.

Black and Peacock Spider Variant
This fly, popularized and even perhaps invented by Tom Ivens, the doyen of still-water flyfishing in Britain, has been responsible for the demise of many thousands of trout. In its original form it was simply dressed with an under-

body (to fatten it) of floss silk overwound with bronze peacock herl and with a long-fibred black hen hackle behind the eye.

My variation was made several years ago because I believe that this dark, bulky fly is taken for a number of insects, including Corixa beetles, spiders, snails and some land-bred beetles and other flies, and the hackle in the middle of the body seems more appropriate. The fly is often taken while sinking slowly, and the middle hackle seems to support the fly more naturally in the water as it does so, and has more life when the fly is being fished normally. It is effective from April to the season's end.

HOOK: Partridge round bend, forged, flat down-eye, sizes 14–10.

DRESSING: Wind black nylon tying thread from behind eye to beginning of bend. Tie in silver Lurex, Mylar or tinsel and wind a tag about 3 mm ($\frac{1}{8}$ in) long over wet varnish on the thread. Tie in 7.5 cm (3 in) of any dark floss silk and 7.5 cm (3 in) of fine copper or gold wire and four to six – depending on hook size – strands of bronze peacock herl by the tips, applying a dab of varnish at this point and also to the underbody – coat this liberally, since the floss absorbs varnish – after winding it to within 3 mm ($\frac{1}{8}$ in) of the eye. Twist the herls together in an anti-clockwise direction and wind them clockwise to a point halfway up the shank. Tie down firmly and rib in opposite direction with the wire. Tie down. Tie in by the base a long-fibred, black-dyed hen hackle and wind two or three turns. Tie off. Wind remaining herls to finish body and again rib with the wire. Whip-finish and varnish the head. The hackle should radiate at right angles and should not be stroked backwards towards the bend.

When the hackle is being tied in, make sure that both the herls and ribbing wire are tied down facing towards the hook eye, so that they may be wound to finish the body without forcing the hackle out of shape.

Shrimp: fishing period, whole season.

HOOK: Partridge Limerick down-eye, size 12.

DRESSING: Wind underbody of either copper wire, or fine lead wire, or wrapped lead foil from a wine bottle top to form a spindle shape. Wind brown or green tying thread from behind eye to slightly round bend, covering wire or lead and securing it. Lead or wire is made more secure after winding by a drop of Super Glue 3. Tie in at bend fine gold wire and dub thread with a mixture of wild rabbit guard hairs and dull orange seal fur in proportions of 70:30 and wind fat body. Rib with wire. Whip-finish behind eye and varnish.

This fly is always fished fairly deeply on a floating line and suitable length of leader and moved in short jerks with pauses between.

Dry flies

Cranefly: fishing period, late July to end of September.

HOOK: long-shank, forged bend; round bend, flat or Limerick, 10, 12.

DRESSING: Wind brown tying nylon from behind eye to beginning of bend and tie in four ruddy fibres from cock pheasant centre tail feather, or buff coloured turkey tail fibres, or condor. Varnish thread and wind body to within 4.5 mm

($\frac{3}{16}$ in) of the eye. Keep body slim and tapered towards bend. Tie overhand knots in centres of six cock pheasant centre tail fibres and tie in by their butts, three on each side of the hook shank and trailing towards the bend. Tie in ginger or light red slim hackle points from a game cock, each about 19 mm ($\frac{3}{4}$ in) long, on top of hook and spread to form a V shape with figure-eight windings over and between them, then return thread to behind wings. Tie in short-fibred matching cock hackle by the butt and wind two turns behind wings, then through them, and two turns in front. Bring thread under tension through hackle and between wings, taking care not to tie in hackle fibres or disturb wing setting, whip-finish at eye and varnish.

Other suggested standard dry fly patterns (sizes in brackets): Black Gnat (14), Coch-y-Bondhu (12, 14), Iron Blue (14, 16), Tup's Indispensable (14, 16), Pheasant Tail (12, 14), Walker's Sedge No. 2 (12, 10), Grey Duster (14); Muddler Minnow (10, normal shank and 8, long shank) for wake fishing, greased.

Lures

White Marabou: fishing period, June to October, at dusk and onwards.
HOOK: Partridge lure hook, sizes 8–12.
DRESSING: Wind white thread from behind eye to opposite barb and tie in bunch of hot orange dyed cock hackles as tail, extending 6 mm ($\frac{1}{4}$ in) behind bend, and white medium-width chenille and fine oval silver tinsel. Wind chenille to within 4.5 mm ($\frac{3}{16}$ in) of eye, rib in opposite spiral with tinsel. Tie in a bunch of white marabou plumes as a bushy wing, to extend to just behind hook bend, then tie in a false hackle of hot-orange dyed cock hackle fibres to extend no more than 6 mm ($\frac{1}{4}$ in). Whip-finish and varnish a bold head with black varnish, applied with fine brush.

Black Marabou: fishing period, April to October, at any time.
HOOK: as for white version.
DRESSING: Exactly the same as the white version, except that the chenille and marabou plumes are black.

Partridge's new lure hooks are an excellent shape and have a small ring instead of an up- or down-turned eye. Good for lures, long-bodied nymphs and seatrout.

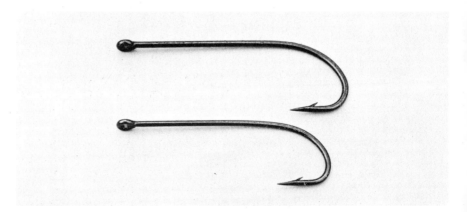

Vulture: fishing period, August and September, whenever roach fry are being attacked by big trout.

HOOK: Partridge lure hook, sizes 12–8, or any strong long-shank hook, 10–6.

DRESSING: Wind white thread from behind eye to opposite barb, then tie in a bunch of hot-orange dyed cock hackle fibres to extend 9 mm ($\frac{3}{8}$ in) behind bend as a tail. Tie in fine oval silver tinsel and white chenille, and wind chenille over varnished underbody to within 4.5 mm ($\frac{3}{16}$ in) of eye and rib in opposite spiral with tinsel. Tie in beard hackle of bunch of hot orange dyed cock hackle fibres, extending underneath hook and round sides for about 6 mm ($\frac{1}{4}$ in). Match two vulturine guinea-fowl hackle feathers (these have white centres, merging to black and with electric-blue tips – and are rather expensive!) for length, so they extend nearly the length of the hook behind the bend, and back to back, and tie them in so that each butt is lying to one side of the hook shank. Varnish the butts and silk, trim off excess quill, then wind a bold head and varnish it red with a small brush.

I produced this pattern initially for fry-feeding trout at Grafham Water in late summer and Dave Collyer, the professional dresser, immediately suggested dressing it matuka-style, to avoid the wings twisting round the hook-bend in casting. The matuka style of dressing involves the wings being tied down along the top of the fly's body with spiral windings of the ribbing tinsel.

Other suggested lures, standard patterns, sizes in brackets, are: Whisky (12–10), Ace of Spades (8 and 6), Price's Orange Streamer (8 and 10), Geronimo (10), Yellow Fellow (10 and 8), Wormfly (12, 10, tandem).

Other recommended traditional lake flies: Invicta (10 and 12), Rogan's Golden Olive (10 and 12), Black Pennell (14–10), Dunkeld (14–10), Cinnamon and Gold (10 and 12), Black and Orange (10 and 12), Lurex Spider (10 and 12), March Brown (14–10).

Dry flies for river trout

My dry fly philosophy being that general colour tone, size and good presentation are more important than having a vast collection of the so-called 'exact imitation' patterns for trout on running water – including chalk-streams – sees me generally fishing with four hackled (wingless) patterns I dreamed up, plus one or two standard dressings that have stood the test of time.

Here are my four faithfuls. They are dressed on size 14 and 16 Partridge up-eye wide gape trout hooks.

Number One: fishing period, all season; good April/May/September.

DRESSING: Wind medium-brown thread to opposite hook point, and there tie in three or four fibres from pale ginger cock hackle, 7.5 cm (3 in) of primrose-yellow tying *silk* and two fibres of the blue-grey herl from a heron's quill feather. The cock hackle fibres should point downwards to form the tail, and be no more than 9 mm ($\frac{3}{8}$ in) long. Wind tying thread to near eye, varnish turns and wind heron herls to form slightly tapered body. Rib in opposite spiral with yellow silk, about five turns. Tie in ginger cock hackle by butt and wind three or four turns. Whip-finish and varnish.

Number Two: fishing period, July to season's end.

DRESSING: Wind black tying thread down shank and tie in opposite the hook point three or four dyed black fibres from a cock hackle as a tail and two strands of dyed purple swan herl, plus a 7.5 cm (3 in) length of medium-brown tying *silk*. Wind herls to halfway up shank and tie off. Tie in ruddy brown cock pheasant centre tail fibres (two) and wind to near eye. (Both over wet varnish.) Rib both colours with brown silk. Tie in short-fibred cree cock hackle and a similar size cream or pale badger cock hackle. Wind together for three turns, whip-finish and varnish head.

Number Three: fishing period, all season.

DRESSING: Wind ruby-red tying *silk* from behind eye to opposite hook point and there tie in three or four fibres from a black-dyed cock hackle. Wind silk forward for just under 3 mm ($\frac{1}{8}$ in) to form a kind of tag, then tie in black-dyed swan, condor or turkey tail herls and wind over wet varnish to within 3 mm ($\frac{1}{8}$ in) of eye and, holding them there with hackle pliers, rib the herls with the tying silk. Tie in a short-fibred, black-dyed cock hackle and wind two turns. Tie in a cream or white cock hackle of the same size, wind two turns in front of the black hackle, tie off and whip-finish and varnish.

Number Four: fishing period, all season.

DRESSING: Wind primrose-yellow tying *silk* to a point opposite hook point and tie in three or four pale ginger cock hackle fibres as a tail, projecting about 6 mm ($\frac{1}{4}$ in). Tie in buff-coloured condor herls, or turkey tail fibres of same colour, and wind to within 3 mm ($\frac{1}{8}$ in) of eye over wet varnish. Rib in opposite spiral with the tying silk. Tie in pale ginger or pale cree short-fibred cock hackle and wind three turns. Tie off, whip-finish and varnish.

These four patterns, which may well have names and are unlikely to be originals, have served me well, but there are many excellent dry fly patterns that other fishermen may well feel the need to carry in their boxes. Among them, I would suggest the following:

Gold-ribbed Hare's Ear (14, 12), Ginger Quill (14, 16), Kite's Imperial (14, 16), Lunn's Caperer (14, 12), Beacon Beige (14, 16), Grey Duster (14, 16), Shadow Mayfly (12), White Wulff and Grey Wulff (14, 12), Greenwell's Glory (12–16).

Seatrout flies

In addition to the two estuary (saltwater) lures, the dressings of which are given in Chapter 7, I suggest the following:

Hugh Falkus' Medicine (10–6), Hugh Falkus' Sunk Lure (tandem hooks, total length 2–3 in), Hugh Falkus' Surface Lure (wake fly – size 6 or 8 tandem hooks, or size 10 tail treble and size 6 belly hook), Teal, Blue and Silver (12–8), Mallard and Claret (12–6), Silver Invicta (12–6), Dunkeld (12–6), Connemara Black 10–6). For small fish (900 g/2 lb) I would add a few of the spider-type flies, such as Black Pennell (14 and 12), Lurex Spider (14 and 12), Silver March Brown (14 and 12) and Partridge and Orange (14 and 12). For dry fly fishing, any palmer-dressed sedge pattern will prove useful, such as a Cinnamon

Sedge, size 12–8, or Peter Deane's Shadow Mayfly. A Blue Zulu dressed with a good, stiff cock hackle, size 10 or 8, is also good.

Salmon flies

Spring fishing recommendations (these are all hair-wing flies on tubes or Waddington mounts, lengths in brackets):

Yellow Dog (3.8–7.5 cm/1½–3 in), Thunder and Lightning (3.8–7.5 cm/1½–3 in), Hairy Mary (5–7.5 cm/2–3 in), Orange Dog (3.8–8.8 cm/1½–3½ in). Note that these tubes are for sunk-line fishing in cold, heavy water.

A plastic tube with a rubber extension fitted to it, and finished tube flies, with hooks in position.

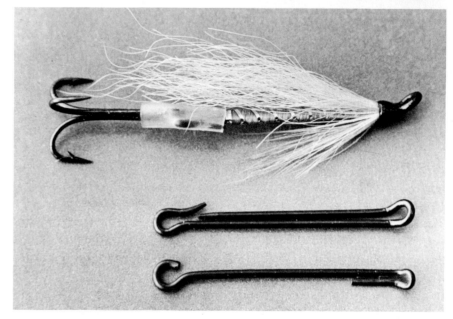

The Waddington mount can produce a very slim fly with the advantage of a replaceable treble hook. The top of the two mounts is the newer design: the hook is put on and the loop is held firm with a few turns of soft wire; the ends of the wire are then twisted together to secure the join.

Late spring and summer recommendations (these are mostly for floating-line and sink-tip fishing when the water is lower, and above about 10°C/50°F):

Jeannie (low water 6 and 8), Blue Charm (low water 4–8), Thunder and Lightning (low water 4–8), Logie (low water 4–8), Hairy Mary (low water 10–6), General Practitioner (low water, doubles 4–8), Roe Purple (low water singles and doubles 10–6), Silver Shrimp (low water singles and doubles 10–6).

Very small flies for low water and bright conditions in high summer, and for grilse:

Jeannie (low water 10 single and 12 double), Silver Shrimp (low water 10 single and 12 double), Stoat's Tail (low water 10 single), Silver Blue (low water 10 single, 10–14 doubles and long-shank Drury trebles), Orange Charm (low water 10 and 8 singles, 14 and 12 doubles).

Special Esox-it pike fly

HOOK: long-shank, forged, size 8–4.

DRESSING: Wind black tying thread from behind eye to opposite barb and tie in a short tail of scarlet fluorescent floss (two or three plies placed together) and oval silver or narrow flat *metal* tinsel. Wind tying thread to within 4.5 mm ($\frac{3}{16}$ in) of eye and tie in black Marabou floss silk. Wind silk to bend and then back over itself again to where it was tied in, forming a tapered body. Rib in opposite spiral with tinsel. Tie in as a false hackle, first a bunch of hot-orange cock hackle fibres followed by – over the top of the orange – a bunch of bright blue hackle fibres. For the wing tie in, in this order and separately, a slim bunch of bright yellow bucktail, or squirrel or calf tail, followed by scarlet and then black hair over the top of the yellow. Place a small dab of varnish on the underbody before setting on the yellow hair, and repeat this when tying in the other colours, which will serve to stick the hairs in position. Finally, place a short tuft of white Orlon on each side of the wing and form a bold head; whip-finish and varnish the head black or red, using a small brush. The fibres of the Orlon are fluffed out when the varnish is dry using a needle. The tail should be trimmed to just under 6 mm ($\frac{1}{4}$ in) in length for the largest fly, a little less than that for the smallest.

Other recommended patterns for pike are: Black Marabou, White Marabou or Appetizer, all on long-shank hooks, as for the Esox-it, and similar patterns, on tandem hooks, up to 10 cm (4 in) in length, including one with silver tinsel bodies on both hook shanks and a mixed wing of yellow, orange and black bucktail. The orange is tied in first, followed by the yellow, with the black hair on top.

Recommended books on flydressing and DIY subjects

Fly-dressing, David J. Collyer (David & Charles)
Fly-tying, Denis H. Ardley (Witherby)
Trout flies of still water, John Goddard (A. & C. Black)
Lures for game, coarse and sea fishing, S. W. 'Taff' Price (A. & C. Black)
Rough stream trout flies, S. W. 'Taff' Price (A. & C. Black)
Reservoir and lake flies, John Veniard (A. & C. Black)

Fly-tying problems and their answers, John Veniard and Donald Downs (A. & C. Black)

Fly-dressing materials, John Veniard (A. & C. Black)

The truth about fluorescents, Thomas Clegg (Tom C. Saville Ltd, Nottingham)

The bankside book of stillwater trout flies, Peter Lapsley (A. & C. Black)

Modern trout flies, W. H. Laurie (MacDonald)

A dictionary of trout flies, A. Courtney Williams (A. & C. Black)

Master fly-tying guide, Art Flick (Crown, New York)

Selective trout, Doug Swisher & Carl Richards (Crown, New York)

Salmon flies, Poul Jorgensen (Stackpole)

Practical fishing knots, Mark Sosin & Lefty Kreh (Crown, New York)

Rod building, Alan Vare & Kenneth Whitehead (Rod & Gun Publishing)

Appendix
Knots

Splicing a plastic-coated flyline to braided nylon shooting line:

1 The end of the line is dipped in cellulose thinners to soften the vinyl, which can then be removed by pinching and drawing it off with finger and thumb nails. This leaves the line's thin braided core exposed.

2 Then a needle is inserted for about 2.5 cm (1 in) into the end of the braided nylon monofilament shooting line. The unravelling may be halted by passing a red-hot needle round the base of the unravelled section while still on the needle, which melts and then fuses the strands together.

3 The core of the flyline is threaded into a needle and drawn into the hollow centre of the shooting line and out, at least 12 mm (½ in) back.

4 Super Glue 3 is used – just two tiny drops – to secure the lines together. An alternative is to use quick-setting epoxy glue which should be applied to the flyline core before it is pulled into the shooting line.

5 If the hot-needle process was not necessary, the unravelled strands are slipped off after gluing.

6 The finished neat splice and the equipment used to make it. The author has never been let down by this splice.

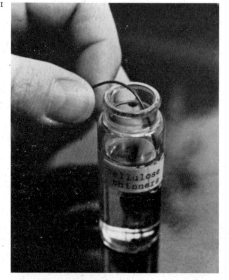

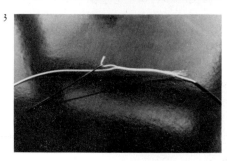

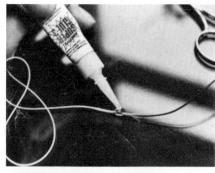

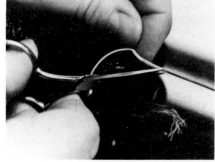

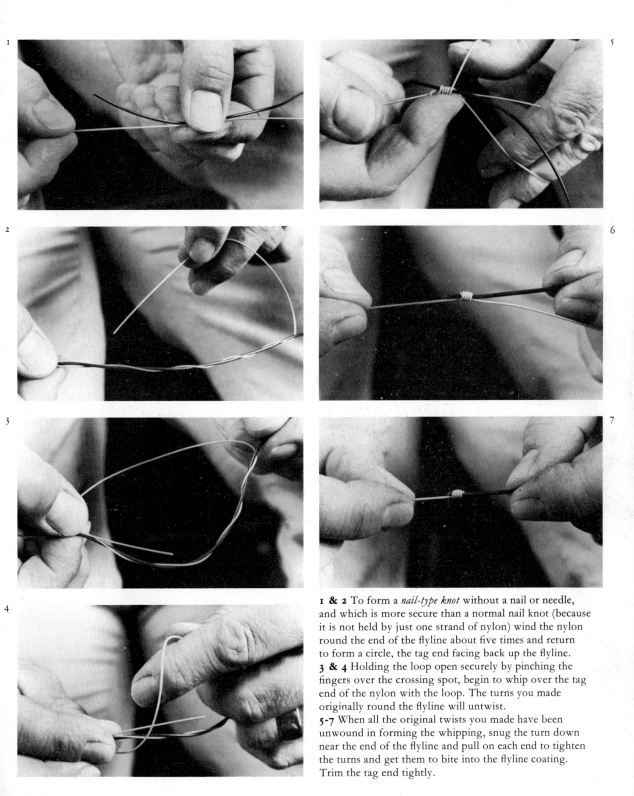

1 & 2 To form a *nail-type knot* without a nail or needle, and which is more secure than a normal nail knot (because it is not held by just one strand of nylon) wind the nylon round the end of the flyline about five times and return to form a circle, the tag end facing back up the flyline.

3 & 4 Holding the loop open securely by pinching the fingers over the crossing spot, begin to whip over the tag end of the nylon with the loop. The turns you made originally round the flyline will untwist.

5-7 When all the original twists you made have been unwound in forming the whipping, snug the turn down near the end of the flyline and pull on each end to tighten the turns and get them to bite into the flyline coating. Trim the tag end tightly.

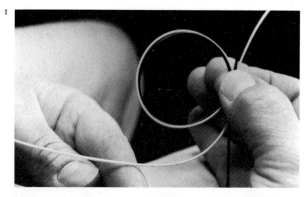

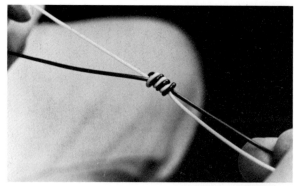

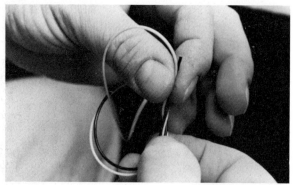

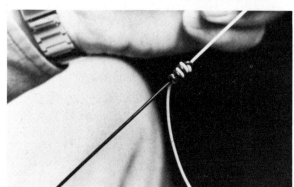

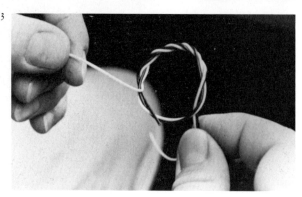

The *four-turn water knot or Cove knot* is simply four over-hand knots, done one after another, and pulling the long tag-end through each time. The final picture shows one end (upper) left as a dropper.

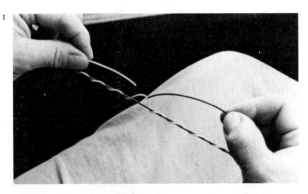

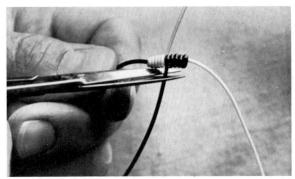

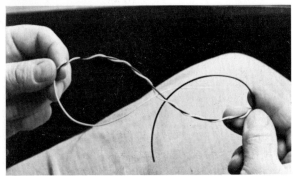

A *blood knot* is made by forming the turns, separating them in the centre so that there are at least five turns either side of the gap, putting the two tag ends through the gap from opposite sides, then pulling on the main parts to tighten the coils.

The *grinner* is more secure for tying on a fly than a tucked half blood (clinch) knot. The twists are made (about four or five) with the tag end, then the end is returned in a loop and passed through the loop the same number of times as the original twists. It is not put through the gap between hook eye and loop, as in the half blood knot, but doing so does seem to increase the strength of the grinner in very thin (below 1.8 kg/4 lb) nylon.

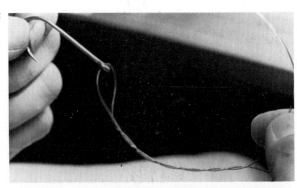

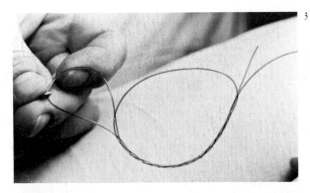

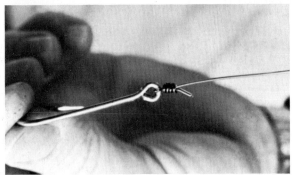

Glossary

Abdomen The slim, tapered rear section of a natural fly's body.

Acid water Water in a river or lake which has an acid content; acid waters usually derive from peaty moorland.

Adipose fin The small, fleshy lobe-like fin between the dorsal and tail (caudal) fins of fish that are members of the salmon family.

AFTMA American Fishing Tackle Manufacturers' Association; in Britain, Association of Fishing Tackle Makers (AFTM). They have standardized weights of flylines for matching to rod actions.

Alkaline water Water rich in calcium, particularly chalk-streams and limestone streams. Rain falling on chalk and limestone filters slowly into the rivers, keeping a fairly constant annual flow, and is characteristically clear. Such waters are rich in insect, crustacean and mollusc life, since they can easily build their shells from the calcium in the environment.

Alevin The newly-hatched young fish, usually referring to the salmonids, which lives for a period on the yolk-sac hanging from its stomach area.

Aluminium oxide A comparatively new material developed in space technology. It is very hard and resists line abrasion when used as a lining in rod rings. Mostly from Japanese sources (Fuji).

Angler's curse A tiny, pale-green upwing fly also known as a Broadwing (scientific name *Caenis*). It hatches in profusion on summer evenings, on rivers and lakes, and often hatches on anglers' clothing. Called 'curse' because fish taking Broadwings are notoriously difficult to catch.

Back-cast Moving the rod, and the line, to the rear, then pausing while the line unrolls in the air before making a forward cast.

Backing line Strong, fine, level rotproof line, usually of Terylene (Dacron is the American term) or braided nylon, but sometimes nylon monofilament, joined to the flyline as a reserve for playing big fish, and to build up the level of the spool hub.

Bag net A landing net with a U-shaped bag, rather than one in a conical shape. Bag nets are more capacious and make removal of fish from them easier.

Beat An area of riverbank, and sometimes of still waters, which is allocated to an angler or anglers for a period of time.

Beard hackle A tuft of the fine fibres stripped off the quill from a chicken's (or other bird's) neck feather and tied in as a bunch below the hook near the eye. Also known as false hackle or throat hackle.

Belly (in line) Usually a curve in the line caused by the current on a river, or wind on a lake. Also used to describe the heavy portion of a flyline where the casting weight lies.

Blank The shaft of material – graphite, glass, cane or other material – forming the basis of a fishing rod. Also used to describe a fishless day – a blank day.

Blowline A thick, gauzy, loosely woven or twisted line, often of silk, used for dapping a fly with the wind's force and a long rod, usually from a drifting boat.

Bobbin-holder A pronged device to hold the bobbin of tying thread under tension when making flies; the thread passes through a thin tube which helps make its application to the hook more precise.

Bobbin-threader A fine, stiff wire loop which is used to thread flydressing tying thread through the bobbin-holder tube.

Boil Fish disturbing the water surface as it takes the fly.

Bonefish *Albula vulpes* A streamlined tropical saltwater fish that inhabits mangrove flats in water between 20 cm (8 in) and 60 cm (2 ft) deep. Much sought by flyfishers and one of the fastest, farthest-running fish in the world for its size.

Bow Often used as an alternative to belly, to describe the curve in a flyline caused by current or wind.

Bucktail Tail hairs from deer, usually American northern whitetail deer, but also fallow deer and others, used to make the wings of flies, especially lures for trout and the wings of salmon flies. The term also means a hair-wing fly on a long-shank hook (American term).

Butt The thick part of a nylon leader; or the part of a rod that is nearest the hand; or the thick part of a feather or feather fibre used in flydressing.

Caddis The larva of a sedge-fly, usually in a case made from vegetable matter, mollusc shells or small stones; caddis grub. American word for sedge-flies.

Caenis A Broadwing fly; see Angler's curse.

Cane Bamboo split into sections, usually hexagonal, then glued together after tapering to form split-cane rod blanks.

Cannibal Term usually used to describe big trout that have taken to feeding mainly on other fish, including small trout.

Carbon fibre Graphitized man-made textile, produced by burning the material in an oxygen-free condition at very high temperatures, used in rod construction. In America – and increasingly elsewhere – the term graphite is used, a shorter but less accurate description of the material.

Cast The action of projecting the flyline; sometimes, but now less frequently used to describe the nylon leader. Going out of flyfishing terminology due to its confusion with the casting action.

Chironomid One of the midges of the non-biting variety, of which there are said to be more than 350 British species (*Diptera* or flat-wing flies).

Coarse fish English term used to describe fish that are not members of the salmon family, including carp, roach, rudd, pike, perch, and so on. In America, called rough fish.

Chenille A soft, plush-like cord into which are twisted fibres of cotton, nylon and other materials, used for the bodies of lure-type flies.

Colour Term used to describe water tinted with mud, peat-stain, and so on, during and after run-off following rain; also used to describe a fish in spawning dress – coloured fish.

Collar A short section of heavier nylon or wire knotted to a leader to connect it to the fly for fish that have sharp teeth or sharp gill-covers, to prevent the leader being severed.

Core The braided level centre of a plastic-coated flyline.

Corixa Term used to describe a water beetle, the Lesser Water Boatman; also describes artificial fly that imitates it.

Cove knot Otherwise known as the four-turn water knot, popularized by well-known British still-water flyfisher, Arthur Cove; used to connect lengths of nylon in a leader and to form strong droppers.

Cover Described the action of casting the fly to a fish or to cast to likely-looking areas of water – to cover the water.

Cranefly The various flat-wing flies known under the general term of daddy-long-legs, of which there are well over 250 British species varying in size from that of large midges to the ones with bodies more than 2.5 cm (1 in) long. Taken by trout and other fish when on surface.

Crustaceans Shrimps, water-lice, water-fleas (*Daphnia*), all food for trout and other freshwater fish.

Dangle A fly is said to be 'on the dangle' when it has swung round in the current and is immediately downstream of the rod; used as a technique in salmon flyfishing.

Dibble The act of making a dropper on a wet-fly leader, or a bushy dry fly, fly, bounce and skim the surface to create a fish-attracting disturbance.

Delivery The act of casting the fly to the fish or to an area of likely water.

Disc-drag A method of applying braking pressure to a reel spool against a running fish, rather like a car disc-brake in appearance; it applies pressure smoothly and in highly variable degrees.

Drag The action of the current causing a bow or belly to form in the line and moving the fly either faster than the current speed or across the current; also the braking mechanism on a reel.

Drift The movement of the surface of still water, caused by wind or changing water temperatures causing a turnover of water; also the passage of a floating fly over a fish or a likely fish-holding spot.

Dorsal Appertaining to the back, usually the main back fin of a fish.

Drogue An underwater parachute or sea-anchor used to slow down the downwind drift of a boat when fishing.

Dropper The short, projecting length of nylon knotted into a leader on which second (or more) flies are attached in wet fly and some nymph fishing.

Dry fly A fly that is fished floating on the surface, generally to imitate a natural fly.

Dub The application of furs and other materials, suitably shredded or chopped into small pieces, to the tying thread, which is made tacky with beeswax; the thread is then wound round the hook-shank to form a fuzzy body.

Easy action The term used to describe a flyrod that bends well down towards the handle – when waved in the air its movements will be like a slow pendulum.

Evening rise Both the hatch of insects that occurs during evenings following warm summer days, and the surface feeding on those flies by the fish.

False cast A casting action, forward in direction, made to gauge the distance and accuracy of the line and fly before dropping the fly on the water on the next cast. It also means back and forward casts to dry a fly, or to increase the speed of the line.

False hackle Another name for the beard or throat hackle.

Fancy flies Wet and dry flies, often with some bright colours in their make-up, that are not specifically meant to copy any particular insect but attract fish due to their general representation of items of food.

Fast-action rod A rod with a stiff lower section and a slim upper section that flexes rapidly when given a sharp wave in the air.

Female ferrule The part of a rod joint into which the thinner section fits (the thinner ferrule is known as the male ferrule). Applies to metal and spigot joints.

Fibres Term used to describe single hair-like pointed strands forming the two sides of a bird's feather, standing out from the central quill, i.e., hackle fibres, wing quill fibres.

Figure-eight The method by which flyline is recovered into the free hand – the hand not holding the rod – when fishing the fly. The line is coiled by fingers and thumb in figure-eight coils; also used to describe a winding of flydressing thread, wound in that way to hold the wings of an artificial fly in a predetermined position.

Fish To fish the fly means to cast and either let the river's current carry it, or to recover it by taking in line, as in still-water fishing and in river fishing.

Floss A twisted thin cord, of silk or man-made fibres, used to form the bodies of many types of artificial fly; also used as a blowline when dapping a fly using a long rod, aided by the wind.

Flotant A preparation, generally oily or in solid form, which is applied to dry flies and to some lines, to make them float high on the water. Flotants come in bottles, as a liquid, in aerosols, or in solid form in tins.

Fluorescent materials Materials, either man-made fibres or natural furs, feathers, and so on, which have been dyed with chemicals so that they absorb atmospheric ultra-violet light and re-emit it as perceived light of startling colour. Reds, oranges, yellows, greens, blues and whites are most used in flies; some floating flylines are also fluorescent, for visibility on the water.

Foul-hook To hook a fish in any part of its body other than its mouth, either accidentally or, as poachers do, deliberately.

Four-turn water knot Also known as the Cove knot, after Arthur Cove, the British flyfisher who popularized it. It is simply four overhand knots, tied one after the other, in two pieces of nylon laid side by side, to join them safely.

Fry Small fish, usually the young of any fish; flies used to simulate them are sometimes known as fry-flies.

Fresh-run A term used to describe a salmon or seatrout that has been in the river, after swimming in from the sea, for a short time – usually less than a week. Fish that have been in freshwater for only forty-eight hours or so will have sea-lice on them – small flat-bodied parasites stuck to the scales, generally near the tail.

Fuji A proprietory Japanese name in the tackle-making business, famous for rod rings with hard centres made from aluminium oxide.

Fuller's earth A soft, brown clay which has grease-absorbing qualities, used in flyfishing to wipe down leaders to make them sink quickly through the surface film of the water; it is often mixed into a putty with washing-up liquid (detergent).

Gaff A strong hook, unbarbed, fitted to a shaft and which is used to lift big fish, usually salmon, from the water when they have been played-out by the fisherman.

Gillie A professional man who helps fishermen, by rowing them to fish from boats, or shows them where fish lie in a river, selects their flies and lands the fish for them.

Glass Term used in fishing to describe glass-reinforced plastic constructions, usually tubular but sometimes solid, from which rods are made.

Glide Smooth, fast-flowing water that is being sucked out of a pool on a river by the mass of water moving downstream. Glides are usually at the tails of pools and are often the fastest-flowing places, faster than the broken water of streams and rapids that appear more boisterous. The riverbed beneath a glide is generally hard, smooth gravel or shillets.

Golden pheasant A bird with highly coloured plumage used in dressing salmon, seatrout and traditional lake trout flies, such as golden pheasant tippets (orange and black feathers used mainly for tails), red breast feathers (for salmon fly hackles), orange rump feathers (for shrimp flies) and crest feathers (toppings) used as salmon, seatrout and lake trout fly tails, the latter being bright, scintillating yellow.

Graphite A term used interchangeably with carbon fibre (see entry under carbon fibre.

Greased-line fishing Outdated term used to describe fishing with a floating line (greased silk in the past) and small subsurface fly for salmon in late spring and summer. Now usually called floating-line fishing.

Grilse A salmon making its first return to the river after a year and part of a summer spent feeding at sea. Size varies from about 1.8–3.6 kg (4–8 lb), averaging around 2.2 kg (5 lb).

Grinner A knot used for tying flies or any item of tackle with an eye or a ring to nylon monofilament leader. It is measurably stronger than any other knot used for this purpose.

Grown-on A fish stocked at a small size which has fed and grown to a good size in the fishery.

Guard hairs The long hairs projecting beyond the soft underfur on many animals, used in dubbing fly bodies or, in some cases, as wings and tails of flies.

Hackles Long, narrow feathers on the necks of chickens and other birds, used to wind round flies, to float them or give them a semblance of life. Cock hackles are bright and stiff; hen hackles are dull and soft. Also used to describe that part of the fly formed behind the eye, either from chicken (or other birds') hackle feathers or feathers from other parts of birds, such as the elbow of a wing.

Hackle pliers Spring-loaded implement used to grip hackles when winding on the fly, or other delicate materials.

Hair-wing fly A fly with a wing or wings of animal hairs.

Hands Usually set in quotation marks, the word describes the ability to use manual dexterity, when fishing, but especially when playing a big fish on light tackle.

Hatch The moment of eclosion when a fly changes from a nymph or pupa to a winged fly; a large number of insects so doing is called a hatch.

Head The top of a pool on a river where the water comes in from the tail or glide of the pool above; usually fairly deep, streamy water and fairly narrowly confined.

Herls Fibres taken from wings, shoulders and tails of birds – such as peacock tails, swan shoulders, wings – to generally wind round the hook to form a furry-looking body.

Hooks Many types and shapes are used in flyfishing. Long-shank hooks have extended shanks for lures and other long-bodied flies; some have upturned eyes, others down eyes, others straight eyes (ringed). Double hooks have a second hook, brazed at the shanks, so that the bends form a V shape. Treble hooks have three hooks brazed together with their bends forming a triangle.

Tandem hooks are two hooks, brazed together, or whipped to nylon, so that one hook is directly in line with the other – some have the front hook upward-facing, but this is wrong and spoils the way a fly fishes, by overbalancing it. Most salmon fly hooks are enamelled black.

Imitative fly One that is dressed to resemble, as closely as possible, the natural insect, crustacean or small fish that is being represented.

Jungle cock An Indian jungle fowl with long hackle feathers of black, orange and white which have a shiny surface, as if painted. They are used to make the cheeks of many salmon flies, and on other fancy flies for seatrout and still-water trout. The importation of these feathers is now banned in Britain, but there are alternatives from other birds, notably the guinea-fowl, which can be used.

Kelt A salmon, seatrout or trout that is debilitated after spawning.

Knotless taper A nylon leader that is tapered from a thick butt, for attachment to the line, down to a slim tippet, without the inclusion of knots.

Kype The hook that appears on the lower jaw of the male salmon, sea trout and trout during the spawning period. It is used to fight with as the cock fish protect spawning territories.

Larva Usually the stage after the egg in some insects, including the sedge flies and midges, and before the pupal stage. The term is also used to describe very young fish soon after hatching from the egg.

Land-bred or terrestrial flies Flies that hatch out on land, such as the craneflies and bluebottles, and which only reach the water when blown there by the wind – flies with no water-life in their young stages.

Lateral line The distinct line down the sides of fish in which are sensory organs.

Leader The length of nylon connecting flyline to fly.

Leaded fly A fly, usually some form of nymph, pupa, larva or shrimp imitation, which has lead wire or sheet, or copper wire, wound round its shank under the body dressing so that the fly sinks quickly to a good depth.

Lee shore The shore towards which the wind is blowing; the shore from which the wind blows is the windward shore, and many people confuse the terms.

Lie A place where a fish rests in a river, particularly a salmon. Salmon passing up a river lie in the same places, year after year, provided they are not drastically changed by floodwater.

Limestone river A river whose course runs mostly through limestone, although more particularly its headwaters; an alkaline river rich in life.

Limerick A word used to describe the shape of the bend in a hook; the point is straight. There are many other such terms used to describe hook shapes.

Loop The shape of the flyline when being projected through the air by the caster; fast-action rods tend to cast narrow loops, slow-action rods wide loops, although the loop may be varied by the caster. Also the loop in some leader butts for attachment to the flyline.

Lunn William Lunn was a famous chalk-stream (River Test) keeper and the inventor of fly patterns including Lunn's Caperer, Lunn's Particular, Houghton Ruby and a few others.

Low-water hook A salmon hook made from finer wire than normal salmon hooks, and intended for dressing sparse, slim flies for use in late spring and summer near the surface on a floating or sink-tip line.

Lure A long-winged, long-bodied fly, on a long-shank single hook or on tandem hooks, used mainly for still-water trout, but is also used for deep fishing for seatrout.

Lurex A plastic film, usually sold on spools in strip form, that looks like shiny gold, silver, blue and copper (among other colours) metal. Used for ribbings and 'tinsel' bodies on flies. It is rather delicate and easily torn by a fish's teeth, but unlike true metallic tinsels, it does not tarnish.

Male ferrule The part of a rod joint which is inserted into the female part (see Female ferrule).

Marabou Fluffy feathers from the legs of turkeys used to make mobile wings on many flies, especially still-water lures. Also the brand name of flydressing silk floss for bodies.

Matuka A style of dressing a lure or other fly on a long-shank hook in which the tinsel used to rib the body is also used to tie down the hackle wing, which projects behind the hook bend.

Mayfly The biggest of the upwing flies (*Ephemeroptera*) in Britain, usually hatching in late May/early June, at which period the larger trout feed avidly on them. In America, the term is used to describe all the upwing flies.

Mend Term describing the way in which the floating – or just subsurface – flyline is transposed by the fisherman, usually in an upstream or upwind (on still water) direction, to prevent the fly being fished too fast.

Midges The flat-wing non-biting *Chironomid* flies forming a major part of the diet of still-water trout.

Milt The sperm-carrying fluid emitted by male fish to fertilize the eggs of the female.

Mites Small members of the spider order having four pairs of legs. Found widely in still waters and mainly coloured red, amber or green. The largest is red and is often found in trout, its body being about 6 mm ($\frac{1}{4}$ in) long.

Monofilament A single strand, usually referring to nylon line used to make leaders.

Muddler Minnow A large artificial fly, dressed on a long-shank hook and characterized by a large, cylindrical head made from deer body hair tied in with thread and then radiated round under tension. It is packed tightly and afterwards trimmed to shape with scissors. Deer hair is buoyant and floats the fly well. Inventor: Don Gapen of America.

Natural Reference to the actual insect as opposed to an artificial fly of the same name, i.e., Mayfly – 'the natural' as opposed to the fly pattern.

Nymph The stage after the egg of flies of the order *Ephemeroptera*, whose life-cycle is egg, nymph, dun, spinner; also the term used to describe the artificial fly to represent nymphs, and a loose term for all wingless fly dressings.

Nymphing Fishing with an artificial nymph; also the action of a trout when taking nymphs.

Nylon A polymer textile from which monofilament lines and leaders are made; also used to make braided lines for shooting lines and backing.

Olives Several species of these upwing flies exist, i.e., Pond Olive, Lake Olive, Blue-winged Olive.

Ova Collective name for the eggs of fish.

Palmer To wind a hackle feather along the shank of a fly hook instead of just behind the eye, usually as an aid to flotation and particularly on sedge imitations; also used in pattern descriptions of flies dressed in this style – Red Palmer, Black Palmer, etc.

Parr The stage following the alevin in the life-cycle of a young salmon, seatrout or trout.

Partridge hooks Hooks made by the Redditch-based company of that name which specializes in hand-made hooks.

Pattern Description of the make-up of an artificial fly, giving materials used and how they are applied.

Pawl A spring-loaded tooth, usually V-shaped, which engages in the teeth of the ratchet wheel on a reel spool and provides a means of resistance to line being pulled off.

Pellets Small lumps of high-protein food used for feeding trout in hatcheries.

Point Either the point of a hook or an English word, now going out of use, meaning the tippet of a fly leader; also, to be 'pointed' by a fighting fish means that the rod is dragged down to the lie along the same plane as the line, without being bent and thus being unable to absorb sudden shocks.

Polypropylene A man-made fibre with a specific gravity less than that of water, which means that it is very buoyant. It is supplied in various forms, including as a yarn, in random pads, like cotton wool, and in sheets. Many colours exist and the material is excellent as the dubbed body of many floating flies, or for flies for fishing just beneath the surface.

Pool Describes the places in salmon rivers where fish lie and where fishing is effective – both conditions are not always met in other places. Pools on good salmon beats are often marked by pegs in the bank, to guide fishermen.

Popping-bug An American surface lure with a buoyant cylindrical head of plastic foam, balsa wood or cork just behind the hook eye, with the rest of the hook being dressed with wings. Used for black bass and other fish in America, they are good for wake fishing, especially in dusk and darkness, for still-water trout and seatrout respectively.

Pre-waxed thread A fine nylon flydressing thread which comes ready-coated with beeswax or other tacky wax on spools. The wax helps materials applied to the hook to stay in place and is essential when applying dubbing to the thread.

Prick To lightly and momentarily engage the hook point in a fish's mouth, then have it come out again; the term is most commonly used in salmon fishing.

Priest A small, heavily-weighted cudgel used to kill fish humanely; comes from 'administering the last rites'.

Pull The action of a fish taking the fly, then letting go again, usually part of salmon-fishing terminology. A fish which does this, without feeling the hook (being pricked) may take the fly again, within minutes, or later the same day.

Pupa The stage following the larva in the life-cycle of some insects; sedge flies and midges are examples of flies which have a pupal stage.

Put-and-take fisheries Fisheries into which trout, usually rainbows, are constantly put as others are taken out, to retain a planned number of fish available for the fishermen.

Rain-fed river A river whose height and rate of flow is largely affected by rainfall, as opposed to chalk-streams, whose waters remain at a fairly constant rate of flow, due to rainfall filtering over a period of time through the ground and into the river, usually via springs.

Ranunculus The water-plants known as crowfoots, of which there are species in still and in flowing waters. They are characterized by long, multi-leaved stems with small, white, surface flowers and provide cover and a food larder of insects for fish.

Ratchet The audible check mechanism on a reel.

Recover To retrieve the flyline by pulling it in, in some way.

Retrieve The same meaning as recover.

Ribbing The spiral-wound tinsel, silk or other material forming a segmented pattern on the body of an artificial fly or to hold the body materials secure.

Rise The action of a fish taking a fly – natural or artificial – near to the surface, usually breaking the surface to form a ring or a whorl. Also, the mass repetition of this action by fish when large numbers of insects are hatching out.

Rod-rings The rings that carry the line on the rod, of which there are several different designs used on flyrods, but they are generally snake or low bridge type.

Roll-cast A circular casting movement which projects a flyline without any part of the line passing to the rear of the fisherman, mainly used in salmon fishing.

Run The action of a hooked fish swimming away at speed; also a number of fish, usually salmon or seatrout, moving up a river.

Running line The braided or monofilament line (backing) attached to the back-end of a flyline as a reserve with which to play large fish.

Sedges The roof-wing flies (caddis-flies in America) that mainly hatch in the evenings; also marsh plants with long, slim stems living in acid soils.

Shooting line The thinner line behind the head or belly of a weight-forward flyline, and the thin braided or monofilament line behind a shooting-taper flyline. Also, the action of letting such line go in casting.

Shrimp Usually the freshwater shrimp, *Gammarus pulex* or *Gammarus lacustris*, which are the most common species of these crustaceans, or an artificial fly to represent these, or a salmon fly dressed to represent the saltwater shrimp.

Sideplates The two discs forming the spool or drum of a reel and situated at each end of the hub.

Smolt The salmon or seatrout after being a parr, and its thumbprint markings on the flanks having changed into a bright silvery coat, when it is ready to migrate to sea.

Spate river A river largely affected by rainfall and up which salmon and seatrout run only when the river is briefly in spare or flood. Fishing on such rivers is usually only good for a brief period while the spate falls.

Spey-cast A development of the roll-cast involving an extra movement of the rod from upstream to downstream before making the forward roll-type cast. Named after the River Spey where its use is so often necessary due to the nature of the high banks behind the caster.

Spider-type flies Wet flies without wings, especially the small, sparsely-dressed north of England flies.

Spigot The type of joint on hollow-glass and graphite rods in which a reduced-diameter section of the material from which the rod is made fits into the tubular part of the other section, to join them.

Spliced rod A split-cane or greenheart wooden rod whose sections are joined by mating opposing tapered, flat areas and then taping them together. Prevents sections turning when casting, as metal ferrules tend to do on salmon rods, where this joint is normally used.

Split cane Bamboo split into sections and planed on the inside into a V shape, then glued together, usually in six sections, to form a solid rod blank.

Spinner The final mature winged stage of an upwing fly after the dun stage.

Streamer A hackle-winged fly dressed on a long-shank hook; also long-stemmed waterplants in running water, such as *ranunculus*, which stream out in the current.

Stock-fish Trout reared in captivity and stocked into fisheries.

Stock pond A pool in which trout and other fish are held while being fed to stocking size.

Strip The action of taking in line by pulling it in with the hand not holding the rod, against tension applied with the forefinger of the rod hand by pressing the line gently against the cork handle.

Squirrel hair Usually the hair from the tail of a squirrel, either an ordinary grey squirrel or one of the others with hair of different colours, used as wings on many types of flies; it may be used in its natural colours or bleached and dyed.

Subsurface The level of water just below the surface down to about 15 cm (6 in).

Sunk line A flyline that is fished well below the surface to within 2.5 cm (1 in) or so of the river or lake bed.

Tag A short, thick tail on an artificial fly, usually made with silk or coloured filaments of nylon; also the turns of tinsel or silk applied to the back-end of the hook on a salmon fly. Can also describe an identifying disc or plastic or metal plate attached to a fish, to trace its migration movements and/or growth.

Tail Has several meanings in flyfishing: the shallow bottom-end of a pool on a river; the slim appendages projecting over the bend of the hook on an artificial fly, and of natural flies which have them. On a leader with a fly or flies on droppers, the fly at the extreme end of the leader is the tail fly.

Tailer A spring-loaded wire loop fixed to a handle which is placed over a salmon's tail when it lies beaten in the edge of the river, to lift it to the bank.

Tandem hooks Two hooks either brazed or whipped together to form the mount for a long-bodied, long-winged fly.

Tarpon A saltwater fish of tropical and sub-tropical waters that also migrates into brackish-water lagoons and canals connected to the sea. Takes the large streamer fly readily and fights by jumping repeatedly; and reaches a weight of at least 127 kg (280 lb).

Terylene A British trade name for a man-made fibre used in fishing lines (Dacron in America).

Test The name of the world's most famous chalk-stream (in Hampshire, England); also the measure of the breaking strain of lines and leaders.

Thorax The front part of an insect's body, thicker than the rear part (the abdomen), which corresponds to the chest in humans.

Throat-hackle The same as a false or beard hackle.

Tighten The act of lifting the rod tip to straighten the line and apply quick tension to it, to sink the hook into the mouth of a taking fish.

Tinsel Metallic or plastic material with shiny silver, gold, copper and other coloured surfaces, used to form the bodies of artificial flies or to rib them to give a segmented effect and add flash in the water. It comes in various thicknesses and in flat, embossed flat, oval and braided or twisted forms. Lurex and Mylar are plastic tinsels.

Tippet The fine tip of a leader, which is often knotted on and replaced as it shortens, so saving the knotless taper; also the orange-and-black barred feathers from the neck of a golden pheasant.

Traditional flies Winged wet flies such as Peter Ross, Invicta, Mallard and Claret, mainly used for seatrout and still-water trout flyfishing.

Treble hook Three hooks brazed together at their shanks and with the bends at equidistant points within a circle, used for tube-flies and Waddington mounts.

Tungsten carbide A man-made metal which is very hard and is used for the abrasion-resistant centres of tip and butt rings for flyrods and for parts of reels which must resist wear.

UDN Ulcerative Dermal Necrosis, a disease affecting salmon, seatrout and brown trout, particularly salmon and seatrout soon after they enter freshwater and especially in cold weather conditions. Little is known about the disease, which has killed millions of fish over the past years in the British Isles since the outbreak in Ireland in 1964.

Upwing flies The *Ephemeroptera*, whose wings are vertical, or nearly so, and which have two or three tails or *setae*.

Upwind Into the wind.

Underbody A thickening of windings of thread, floss or other material beneath the main dressing material on the body of an artificial fly.

Underfur The fine, soft fur beneath the longer fur and guard-hairs on many mammals, used as a dubbing material on artificial flies.

Vice The apparatus used to clamp a hook firmly by its bend while a fly is dressed on its shank.

Waddington mounts Lengths of hardened wire, enamelled black, with an open eye at one end – which takes a treble hook, after which it is squeezed shut – and a loop-eye at the other, for leader attachment. The fly is dressed on the shank. A recent improvement has a clip to take the hook, thereby making replacement easy.

Water-bred flies Flies whose eggs hatch in the water and transpose through various stages until the winged adult hatches at the surface.

Wet fly A fly that is fished beneath the surface of the water and has either wings and a hackle or just a hackle.

Whipping Turns of thread made to attach a ring to a rod blank or finish off the head of a fly, where the end is held under the final turns of thread, to keep all secure.

Windward The direction from which the wind is blowing.

Wings Those of a natural fly and of artificial flies, even the long hair or feather appendages on salmon flies and tube-flies which radiate from around the shank of the hook near the eye or end of the tube and stretch back towards the hook.

Reading list and addresses

Salmon fishing
Salmon, Arthur Oglesby (Macdonald)
Torridge fishery, L. R. N. Grey (Nicholas Kaye)
Secrets of the salmon, Edward R. Hewitt (Charles Scriber's Sons, New York)
Salmon taking times, R. V. Righyni (Macdonald)
Advanced salmon fishing, R. V. Righyni (Macdonald)
Salmon fishing philosophy and practice, Richard Wadding (Faber and Faber)
The Atlantic salmon, Lee Wulff (A. S. Barnes & Co., New York)
Letters to a salmon fisher's sons, A. H. Chaytor (John Murray)
The floating line for salmon and seatrout, Anthony Crossley
A man may fish, T. C. Kingsmill Moore

Trout (in rivers)
Nymph fishing in practice, Oliver Kite (Herbert Jenkins)
Nymphs and the trout, Frank Sawyer (A. & C. Black)
Small river flyfishing for trout and grayling, James Evans (A. & C. Black)
The way of a man with a trout, G. E. M. Skues (Benn)
Nymph fishing for chalkstream trout and *Minor tactics of the chalkstream*, (two books in
    one) G. E. M. Skues (A. & C. Black)
How to fish a Highland stream, John Inglis Hall (G. P. Putnam's Sons)
A summer on the Test, John Waller Hills (Barry Shurlock)

Trout (still water)
Still-water fly-fishing, T. C. Ivens (Andre Deutsch)
Bank fishing for reservoir trout, Jim Calver (A. & C. Black)
Stillwater trout, Brian Harris (Osprey Publishing Ltd)
Reservoir trout fishing, Bob Church (Cassell)
Catching big trout, Alan Pearson (Stanley Paul)
Lake and loch fishing, W. A. Adamson (A. & C. Black)
The pursuit of stillwater trout, Brian Clarke (A. & C. Black)

Seatrout
Sea trout fishing, Hugh Falkus (Witherby)
Salmon and seatrout in wild places, Sidney Spencer (Witherby)

Grayling
Grayling, R. V. Righyni (Macdonald)

General reading
The well-tempered angler, Arnold Gingrich (Alfred A. Knopf, New York)
A flyfisher's life, Charles Ritz (Max Reinhardt)
Trout, Ernest Schwiebert (Andre Deutsch)
Fishing: my life's hobby, Norman McCaskie (Falcon Press)
The complete book of flyfishing, Joe Brooks (A. S. Barnes, New York)
The flies in my hat, Greg Kelly (Hodder & Stoughton Ltd)
Round the bend in the stream, Sir Hudson Fysh (Angus & Robertson)
Trout at Taupo, O. S. Hintz (Max Reinhardt)
Fisherman's paradise, O. S. Hintz (Max Reinhardt)
A fisherman's year, John Parsons (Collins)
Armchair adventures for the angler, edited by Charles K. Fox (A. S. Barnes, New York; Thomas Yoseloff Ltd, London)
Tales of freshwater fishing, Zane Grey (A. S. Barnes, New York)
Fly fishing, Lord Grey of Fallodon (Barry Shurlock)
A gamefisher's year, William B. Currie (Pelham Books)
An incompleat angler, Lord Hardinge of Penshurst (Michael Joseph)
A river never sleeps, Roderick Haig-Brown (William Morrow & Co., New York)

Information
Practical fishing knots, Mark Sosin & Lefty Kreh (Crown Publishers, New York)
Stillwater trout fisheries, edited by H. F. Wallis (Benn)
The fishing waters of Scotland, Moray McLaren & William B. Currie (John Murray)
McClane's standard fishing encyclopaedia, edited by A. J. McClane (Holt, Rinehart & Wilson, New York)
An angler's entomology, J. R. Harris (A. & C. Black)

Useful addresses
John Veniard Ltd, 4–6 High Street, Westerham, Kent (Flydressing materials, tools and tackle)
Sue Burgess Fishing Tackle, Glyn Celin, Felin Fach, Brecon, Powys, Wales (Flydressing materials, tools and tackle – Diamondback rods)
Tom C. Saville Ltd, Princes Works, Station Road, Beeston, Nottingham (Flydressing materials, tools and tackle – a good source of rod kits and fittings)
Dermot Wilson, Nether Wallop Mill, Stockbridge, Hampshire (All tackle, Orvis reels, tuition and fishing)
C. Farlow & Co. Ltd, 5 Pall Mall, London SW1 (Incorporating Sharpes of Aberdeen, makers of fine cane rods – tackle, flies, good service)
Sid Knight, 6 Uplands Drive, Bridgnorth, Salop (Flies, exceptional dry sedges)
Davy Wotton, 29 Camden Road, St Peter's, Broadstairs, Kent (Flies of all types; excellent traditional lake flies)
Robert McHaffie, 33 Glengiven Avenue, Limavady, Co. Londonderry, Northern Ireland (Flies in the Irish style; excellent dry flies and salmon flies)

Index

Figures in *italic* refer to diagrams and illustrations.